Water Sources

PRINCIPLES AND PRACTICES OF WATER SUPPLY OPERATIONS SERIES

Water Sources, Third Edition

Water Treatment, Third Edition

Water Transmission and Distribution, Third Edition

Water Quality, Third Edition

Basic Science Concepts and Applications, Third Edition

Water Sources

Third Edition

American Water Works Association

Science and Technology

AWWA unites the drinking water community by developing and distributing authoritative scientific and technological knowledge. Through its members, AWWA develops industry standards for products and processes that advance public health and safety. AWWA also provides quality improvement programs for water and wastewater utilities.

Project Manager/Senior Technical Editor: Mary Kay Kozyra
Production Editor/Cover Design: Carol Stearns
Production Services: Claro Systems

Disclaimer
Many of the photographs and illustrative drawings that appear in this book have been furnished through the courtesy of various product distributors and manufacturers. Any mention of trade names, commercial products, or services does not constitute endorsement or recommendation for use by the American Water Works Association or the US Environmental Protection Agency. In no event will AWWA be liable for direct, indirect, special, incidental, or consequential damages arising out of the use of information presented in this book. In particular, AWWA will not be responsible for any costs, including, but not limited to, those incurred as a result of lost revenue. In no event shall AWWA's liability exceed the amount paid for the purchase of this book.

Library of Congress Cataloging-in-Publication Data
Water sources.--3rd ed.
      p. cm. -- (Principles and practices of water supply operations series)
   Includes bibliographical references and index.
   ISBN 1-58321-229-9
      1. Water-supply. 2. Water quality. I. American Water Works Association. II. Series.

TD390.W38 2003
628.1'62--dc21   2003050334
                                                                       CIP

ISBN 1-58321-229-9

American Water Works Association

6666 West Quincy Avenue
Denver, CO 80235-3098
303.794.7711

Contents

Foreword

Water Sources is part one in a five-part series titled Principles and Practices of Water Supply Operations. It contains information on water supply sources, the use and conservation of water, source water quality, and source protection.

The other books in the series are

Water Treatment
Water Transmission and Distribution
Water Quality
Basic Science Concepts and Applications (a reference handbook)

References are made to the other books in the series where appropriate in the text.

The reference handbook is a companion to all four books. It contains basic reviews of mathematics, hydraulics, chemistry, and electricity needed for the problems and computations required in water supply operations. The handbook also uses examples to explain and demonstrate many specific problems.

Acknowledgments

This third edition of *Water Sources* has been revised to include new technology and current water supply regulations. Jane Rowan of Schnabel Engineering, Inc., and George Rest of O'Brien & Gere Engineers, Inc., provided coordination and technical review of the revision. The authors of the revision are Paul I. Welle, P.E., senior associate, Schnabel Engineering, Inc., (chapter 1); Mark H. Dunscomb, P.G., senior geologist, Schnabel Engineering, Inc. (chapter 2); John P. Harrison, P.E., Associate Engineer, Schnabel Engineering, Inc. (chapter 3); Lloyd Gronning, P.E., Parsons (chapter 4); Thomas Dumm, P.E., senior project associate, O'Brien & Gere Engineers, Inc. (chapter 5); Harish Aurora, Ph.D., P.E., senior technical associate, O'Brien & Gere Engineers, Inc. (chapter 6); and Jane O. Rowan, P.W.S., associate scientist, Schnabel Engineering, Inc. (chapter 7). Tony Wachinski, Ph.D., P.E., Pall Water Processing, and Bill Lauer, utility quality programs manager, American Water Works Association, provided overall review of the third edition.

The authors of the second edition were R. Patrick Grady, assistant editor, and Peter C. Karalekas Jr., editor, with the *Journal of the New England Water Works Association*. Reviewers of the second edition included Tom Feeley, Eugene B. Golub, William T. Harding, Stephen E. Jones, Kenneth D. Kerri, Gary B. Logsdon, and Garret P. Westerhoff. AWWA staff who reviewed the manuscript included Robert Lamson, Ed Baruth, Bruce Elms, and Steve Posavec. Harry Von Huben served as series editor.

Publication of the first edition was made possible through a grant from the US Environmental Protection Agency, Office of Drinking Water, under Grant No. T900632-01. The principal authors were Joanne Kirkpatrick and Benton C. Price, under contract with VTN Colorado, Inc.

The following individuals are credited with participating in the review of the first edition: E. Elwin Arasmith, Edward W. Bailey, James O. Bryant Jr., Earle Eagle, Clifford H. Fore, James T. Harvey, William R. Hill, Jack W. Hoffbuhr, Kenneth D. Kerri, Jack E. Layne, Ralph W. Leidholdt, L.H. Lockhart, Andrew J. Piatek Jr., Fred H. Soland, Robert K. Weir, Glenn A. Wilson, Leonard E. Wrigley, and Robert L. Wubbena.

Introduction

Supplying water to the public is one of the most important services offered to society by water supply professionals. It has grown in importance and complexity throughout the late nineteenth, twentieth, and early twenty-first centuries. With the advent of the Safe Drinking Water Act, signed by President Ford in 1974, a new era of responsibility dawned for the water utility operator.

Prior to that time, the operator's job was in large part mechanical. He or she kept the pumps running, the valves functioning, and the simple disinfection process from shutting down. The operator changed charts, washed filters, kept the buildings and grounds tidy, and handled a few basic chemicals.

Now the operator does all of those things, but with greater care and greater precision. He must still be a good mechanic, but now, if the job is to be done well, he must also have some basic knowledge of microbiology, chemistry, laboratory procedures, and public relations. The operator must be ready to explain to the community what his job consists of, why water rates seem to rise continually, and that an adequate supply of safe, palatable water is still a great bargain. The operator must reach out to the schools in the service area and teach students of all ages, both in the classroom and at the treatment plant, about the water treatment process. Most important of all, the operator must constantly be aware of public health issues. Any action she takes must be taken only if the public health has been considered. The operator has the potential to create serious health hazards by negligence or to make dangerous situations harmless by using her knowledge and skill.

As is true of any quality product, the raw material is very important. The water utility operator's raw material is the source water. Every source is different, and the operator must become the most knowledgeable, best-informed person about the source or sources he or she is working with. This is true whether the source is a single well, a number of well fields, a spring, a river, or a lake.

This book will introduce the operator to the basic information related to water sources. The operator's goal should always be to take the available source water and perform the functions necessary to supply the customers with a safe, high-quality product.

1

Water Supply Hydrology

Precipitation in the form of rain or snow is the source of water for most surface water supplies.

Hydrology is the science dealing with the properties, distribution, and circulation of water and its constituents in the atmosphere, on the earth's surface, and below the earth's surface. Of particular interest in studying water supply operations are the following:

- how water is constantly replenished by the hydrologic cycle,
- how groundwater supplies are recharged and are available for public water supply use,
- how surface water provides sources of supply for many public water systems, and
- the terms commonly used in the water supply industry to describe the volume and flow of water.

THE HYDROLOGIC CYCLE

The constant movement of water from the surface of the earth to the atmosphere and back again is called the water cycle or, more commonly, the hydrologic cycle. The hydrologic cycle is illustrated in Figure 1–1.

The major steps involved in the hydrologic cycle are as follows:

1. Water moves from earth to sky (evaporation and transpiration).
2. Water vapor forms tiny droplets (condensation).
3. Water falls back to earth (precipitation).

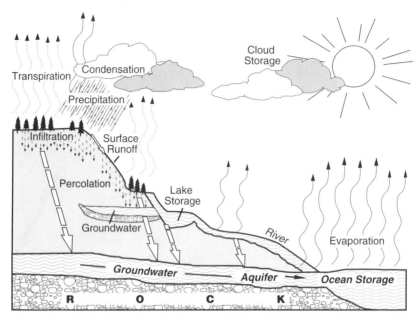

FIGURE 1–1 The hydrologic cycle

4. Some water falls on trees and other vegetation (interception).

5. Water on the earth penetrates the ground or runs off the surface (infiltration, percolation, surface runoff).

These steps are a simplification of a complex interaction between water and the physical world, whether it is in the atmosphere, on the surface, or under the ground. Thus, it is essential to understand the interaction between surface water and groundwater in order to address water supply and water quality issues.

Evaporation and Transpiration

Water moves from the earth to the atmosphere in two ways. One is evaporation. Evaporation occurs when liquid water changes to an invisible gas that circulates into the air. For example, your hands become dry after washing even if you do not use a towel, and a wet driveway dries by evaporation after a rain shower. Heat from the sun speeds the evaporation process. Enormous amounts of water are evaporated from oceans, lakes, and streams, as well as from the land surface. The gas, which is called water vapor, moves through the air above the earth, and when conditions are right, the vapor condenses and clouds are formed.

Another way in which water becomes water vapor and is transferred to the air is transpiration. In this process, water from the earth is absorbed by the roots of plants such as grasses, bushes, and trees. The water moves through the plant, and the blades of grass or the leaves on the trees transfer the water to the air.

Condensation

On a hot summer day, a glass of cold liquid is soon covered with very tiny drops of water that eventually combine and run off the glass. When conditions are right, the same thing happens in the atmosphere. Water vapor condenses and forms clouds, which are large masses of very tiny drops of water or ice crystals. This change from water vapor to water drops is called condensation. Clouds can appear dazzling white or very dark and can have an endless variety of shapes, but they are always made up of water drops or ice crystals.

Precipitation

If enough droplets combine, they become too heavy to stay airborne and fall to the earth as drizzle or rain. If enough ice crystals form to become very heavy, they fall to earth as hail, sleet, or snow. This process is called precipitation. The world's freshwater supply is constantly being redistributed by precipitation.

Infiltration and Percolation

As rain or snow falls on the ground, some of it soaks into the soil. The movement of water through the earth's surface into the soil is called infiltration. The water that soaks into the soil first replaces deficient soil moisture. The water in the root zone of plants can be taken up by the plants to become part of the plant or again be sent into the air by transpiration.

Another portion of the infiltrated water goes back to the surface because of the capillary action of the soil. Capillary action is the force that causes water to rise above a water surface through porous soil. The capillary rise in coarse sand is only about 5 in. (125 mm) but it may be as much as 40 in. (1,000 mm) in some silty soil. Water from beneath the earth's surface can also discharge into the streams, recharging the stream flow.

Most of the remaining infiltrated water continues to move downward below the root zone to a water-saturated area. This downward movement of water is called percolation.

Surface Runoff

When the precipitation rates exceed the infiltration capacity of the soil, the excess precipitation then begins to flow downhill over the surface. This process is called overland runoff or surface runoff.

Most of the surface runoff then flows to a water body such as a wetland, creek, river, or lake, and much of it eventually reaches the oceans. The hydrologic cycle thus continues.

GROUNDWATER

Groundwater is the result of the infiltration and percolation of water down to the water table through the void spaces in the soil and the cracks in consolidated rocks. (See chapter 2 for more information on groundwater sources.) An easy way to visualize groundwater is to fill a glass bowl halfway with sand, as shown in Figure 1–2. If water is poured onto the sand, it infiltrates into the sand and percolates down through the voids until it reaches the watertight (impermeable) bottom of the bowl. As more water is added, the sand becomes saturated and the water surface in the sand rises. The water in this saturated sand is equivalent to a groundwater aquifer. An aquifer is defined as any porous, water-bearing geologic formation.

When the sand in the bowl is partially saturated with water, the level of the water surface can be found by poking a hole or cutting a stream channel in the sand. As illustrated in Figure 1–3, the level of water in the channel is the same as the level of the water surface throughout the sand. This level is called the water table. The water table may also be called the top of the groundwater, the top of the zone of saturation, or the top of the aquifer.

Dry or Unsaturated Soil

Saturated Sand or Other Aquifer Material

FIGURE 1–2 Simplified example of groundwater

Aquifers and Confining Beds

Groundwater occurs in two different kinds of aquifers: unconfined aquifers and confined aquifers.

Unconfined aquifers

When the upper surface of the saturated zone is free to rise and decline, the aquifer is referred to as an unconfined aquifer, or water-table aquifer (Figure 1–4). Wells that are constructed to reach only an unconfined aquifer are usually referred to as water-table wells. The water level in these wells indicates the level of the water table of the surrounding aquifer. The amount of water that the water-table well can produce may vary widely as the water table rises and falls in relation to the amount of rainfall.

FIGURE 1–3 Illustration of a water table

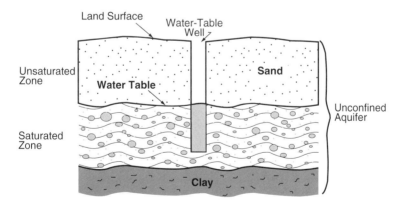

FIGURE 1–4 Cross section of an unconfined aquifer

Confined aquifers

A confined aquifer, or artesian aquifer, is a permeable layer that is confined by an upper layer and a lower layer that have low permeability (Figure 1–5). As illustrated in the figure, the water recharge area (the location where water enters the aquifer) is at a higher elevation than the main portion of the artesian aquifer. As a result, the water is usually under pressure. Therefore, when a well is drilled through the upper confining layer, the pressure in the aquifer forces water to rise up above the confining layer. In some cases, the water will rise above the ground surface, producing a flowing artesian well. In most cases, it will not rise as high as the ground surface and will produce a nonflowing artesian well.

A confining bed is a layer of material, such as consolidated rock or clay, that has very low permeability and restricts the movement of groundwater either into or out of adjacent aquifers.

The height to which water will rise in wells located in an artesian aquifer is called the piezometric surface. This surface may be higher than the ground surface at some locations and lower than the ground surface at other points of the same

FIGURE 1–5 Cross section of a confined aquifer

aquifer. Further discussion of the piezometric surface is provided in the hydraulics section of *Basic Science Concepts and Applications*, part of this series.

There can be more than one aquifer beneath a particular surface area. For instance, there may be a layer of gravel, a layer of clay, another layer of sand or gravel, and another layer with low permeability. Some wells are constructed to tap several different aquifers. In locations where the water quality varies in each aquifer, a well may be constructed to draw water only from the aquifer with the best quality.

Aquifer Materials

Aquifers may be made up of a variety of materials. One characteristic that is important from a water supply standpoint is the porosity, which represents the fraction of void space within a given amount of the material. The porosity determines how much water the material can hold. The other important characteristic is how easily water will flow through the material, known as its permeability, or hydraulic conductivity. Both of these factors determine the amount of water an aquifer will yield. Figure 1–6 illustrates the common aquifer materials.

Aquifers composed of material with individual grains such as sand or gravel are called unconsolidated formations. The range of sizes and arrangement of the grains in the material are important. For example, two aquifers—one composed of fine sand and one of coarse sand—may contain the same amount of water, but the water will flow faster through the coarse sand. A well in the coarse sand can therefore be pumped at a higher rate, and the pumping costs will be less.

Limestone and fractured rock formations are consolidated formations. These formations produce water from channels, fractures, and cavities in the rock. Some fractured rock formations can produce very large quantities of water.

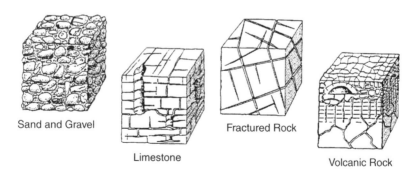

Sand and Gravel

Limestone

Fractured Rock

Volcanic Rock

FIGURE 1–6 Common aquifer materials

Groundwater Movement

Water naturally moves downhill (downgradient) toward the lowest point. In the examples shown in Figures 1–2 and 1–3, the water will not move in any direction because the water table is flat. However, water tables are not usually flat.

Figure 1–7 shows how a water table might actually occur in nature. When rain falls on the watershed, some of the rain infiltrates into the soil and percolates downward to the water table. A mound of water within the aquifer is then built up above the level of the rest of the water table. The water within this mound slowly flows downgradient, increasing the level of the water table slightly and, if the water table is high enough, draining into the stream channel. In most areas, more rain occurs before the mound completely drains off, so the water table never becomes level.

The movement of groundwater is illustrated further in Figure 1–8, in which a cutaway view shows a section of the ground surface. The water table is continuous and sloped, and the groundwater moves downgradient toward the lowest point—the stream channel. In this example, the water table is above the level of the

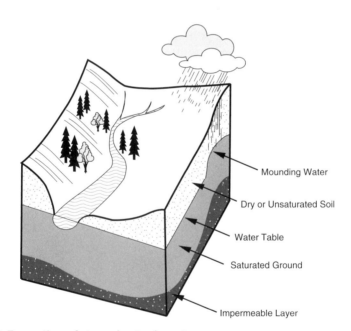

FIGURE 1-7 Formation of groundwater in nature

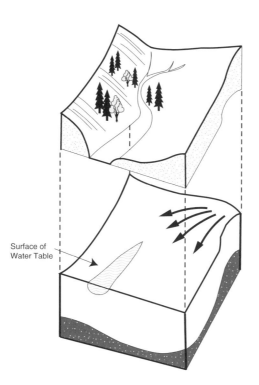

Surface of
Water Table

FIGURE 1–8 Groundwater movement

stream channel. Consequently, water will flow into the stream. But, as explained later, if the water table is below the streambed, water will infiltrate from the stream to the aquifer.

Springs

Springs occur if the water table intersects the surface of the ground or if the water-bearing crevices of fractured rock come to the surface (Figure 1–9). Springs flowing from sand or soil often come from a source that is relatively close. Springs flowing from fractured rock can come from more distant locations, and their origin is usually difficult to determine.

Because of the difficulty in determining where spring water is coming from, springs should generally be considered contaminated until proven otherwise. Many supposed "springs" have stopped flowing when a broken sanitary sewer or septic tank was repaired.

A. Spring resulting from an outcropping of impermeable material

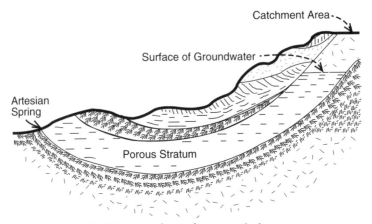

B. Spring resulting from a recharged porous stratum

FIGURE 1-9 Common types of springs

SURFACE WATER

Surface water in lakes and streams provides a source of water for many public water supply systems. (See chapter 3 for more information on surface water sources.) The amount of surface water available varies widely by region of the country and also by season of the year.

The quality of the surface water available for water system use also varies. Some locations are fortunate to have very clean water available, whereas the only available sources in other areas require extensive treatment to make the water safe and palatable for human consumption.

Chemical Constituents of Rain and Snow

Precipitation in the form of rain or snow is the source of water for most surface water supplies. The amount of foreign material in rain and snow is minimal in comparison with the amount that the water will later have after running over or through the ground, but the water is far from chemically pure. Precipitation dissolves the gases in the atmosphere as the water falls to the ground and it also collects dust and other solid materials suspended in the air.

Atmospheric deposition is the process whereby airborne particles and gases are deposited on the earth's surface. Because the particles and gases in the atmosphere are from natural sources such as forest fires, volcanoes, and oceanic salt or from wind-blown soil and materials released into the air from combustion, industrial processes, motor vehicles, and other sources, there is considerable variation in the constituents of rain and snow. But in general, precipitation without the impact of human activities is very soft, is low in total solids and alkalinity, has a pH slightly below neutral (pH 7), and is quite corrosive to most metals. There is considerable variability depending on local conditions. The National Atmospheric Deposition Program monitors the chemistry of precipitation at more than 200 sites nationwide. Data collected by this program indicate that the annual average concentrations of the constituents of precipitation are as follows:

Calcium:	0.02–1.27 mg/L as Ca ions
Magnesium:	4–105 µg/L as Mg ions
Sodium:	15–980 µg/L as sodium (Na ions)
Ammonium:	0.01–0.95 mg/L as ammonium (NH_4 ions)
Chloride:	0.03–1.639 mg/L as chloride (Cl ions)
Sulfate:	0.1–2.6 mg/L as sulfate (SO ions)
Nitrate:	0.2–2.2 mg/L as nitrate (NO_3 ions)
pH:	4.3–6.3
Mercury:	3.6–19.4 ng/L as mercury (Hg)

Source: National Atmospheric Deposition Program 2000 Annual Summary. 2001. Additional data are available at the NADP Internet site: http://nadp.sws.uiuc.edu.

Constituents Added During Runoff

Precipitation that falls on the ground surface and does not infiltrate into the soil or evaporate into the air will travel over the land surface to a surface water body. In the process, a great variety of materials may be dissolved or taken into suspension. Surface water's constituents therefore reflect both the surface characteristics and the geology of the area.

The presence of soluble formations near the surface (such as gypsum, rock salt, and limestone) will have a marked effect on the chemical characteristics of surface water. On the other hand, if the geological formations are less soluble, such as sandstone or granite, the composition of the surface water in the area will tend to be more like that of rain.

If water flowing over the ground surface is exposed to decomposing organic matter in the soil, the carbon dioxide level of the water will be increased. This, in turn, will increase the amount of mineral matter dissolved by the water.

Snow As Water Storage

Snow is a very important form of water storage. Snowmelt greatly prolongs the flow in many streams. If rainfall were the only source of water for surface water bodies, many streams would have very low flows or, in some cases, no flow during dry periods.

Groundwater Augmentation of Surface Water

Figure 1–10 illustrates how stream flow is augmented by groundwater. If the water table adjacent to the stream is at a higher level than the water surface of the stream, water from the water table will flow to the stream. This is referred to as groundwater discharge. Conversely, when the water table is below the stream

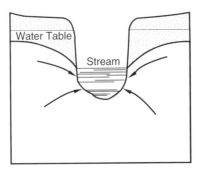

FIGURE 1–10 Surface flow from groundwater seepage

12

surface, water from the stream infiltrates into the ground. The recharge of ground-water from a stream is illustrated in Figure 1–11.

Surface Runoff

The drainage basin or watershed is the land surface that contributes water to area streams and water bodies. The amount and the flow rate of surface runoff through the drainage basin are highly variable, depending on both natural conditions and human influences. In some cases, water is held on the surface for a relatively long time. This is generally good from a water resources standpoint because it allows more water to infiltrate into the ground and recharge groundwater aquifers. If water flows off slowly, it also generally causes less erosion and creates less flooding. At the same time, the longer the water is in contact with the soil, the greater the mineral content of the water will be. Surface water running quickly off land may be expected to have all of the opposite effects.

Surface water runoff flows along the path of least resistance. It begins as sheet flow, then forms rivulets, which flow into wetlands, brooks, creeks, rivers, lakes, and, in some cases, eventually to the ocean. All water that runs off the land flows toward a primary watercourse. The land area of the drainage basin is sloped toward a watercourse. As shown in Figure 1–12, a drainage basin or watershed is surrounded by high ground, or a divide, that separates one watershed from another.

Watercourses

Typical natural watercourses include brooks, creeks, streams, and rivers. There are also many human-made facilities that are constructed to hasten the flow of sur-face water or to divert it in a direction different than it would flow under natural

A. High water table   B. Low Water Table

FIGURE 1–11 Stream flow recharging groundwater

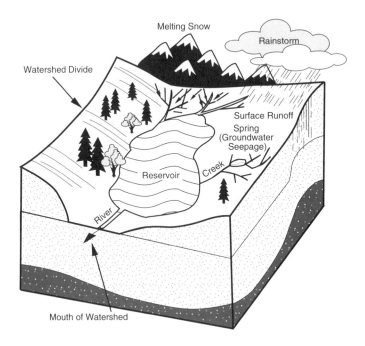

FIGURE 1–12 Schematic of a typical watershed

conditions. Such structures include ditches, channels, canals, aqueducts, conduits, tunnels, and storm sewers.

Water bodies

A water body is a surface water storage basin. It can be a natural basin such as a wetland, pond, lake, or reservoir constructed to serve some specific water need. Reservoirs range from small basins constructed by farmers for watering livestock to massive reservoirs that store water for public water systems, recreation, and/or other uses. Water bodies can have significant impact on the flow and quality of water in streams downstream of the reservoir.

VOLUME AND FLOW

The branch of science that deals with fluids at rest and in motion is known as hydraulics.

Every water system has a number of measurements that must be made, recorded, and filed relating to the rate and amount of water passing through the system. Many of the instruments a water system operator uses are designed so that the instrument "makes" the hydraulic calculation and the operator simply reads the instrument. An example is the water meter. Both the small residential type and the type used in a pump station or a treatment plant are designed so that the volume of water is measured continuously and the total amount of water passing through the meter is indicated in gallons (liters) or cubic feet (cubic meters). Another example is a flowmeter that converts the passage of water through it to a rate of flow. The same instrument frequently makes these two measurements.

A number of terms relate to measuring water. The following paragraphs discuss these terms.

Volume

Volume is the measurement of a quantity of water. In English units, it is most often expressed in gallons, millions of gallons, cubic feet, or acre-feet. In metric units, it is measured in liters, millions of liters, cubic meters, or hectare-meters. A water volume measurement may describe such things as the amount of water contained in a reservoir or the quantity of water that has passed through a treatment plant.

Flow Rate

The measurement of the volume of water passing by a point over a period of time is called the flow rate. Following are some of the units most frequently used for expressing flow rate:

- gallons per minute (gpm) or liters per minute (L/min),
- gallons per hour (gph) or liters per hour (L/hr),
- gallons per day (gpd) or liters per day (L/d),
- million gallons per day (mgd) or megaliters per day (ML/d), and
- cubic feet per second (ft^3/sec) or cubic meters per second (m^3/sec).

Instantaneous Flow Rate

The rate at which water passes by a point at any instant is called the instantaneous flow rate. The instantaneous flow rate through a water plant, for instance, varies constantly throughout the day.

Average Flow Rate

Dividing the total volume of water passing a point by a length of time provides an average flow rate. For instance, most water system reports show the average use for each day in gallons per minute (liters per minute). This is obtained by dividing the total volume of water pumped for the day by 1,440 minutes in a day.

Some other average flow rates that are frequently computed for water supply system operations are

- annual average daily flow,
- peak-hour demand,
- peak-day demand,
- minimum-day demand,
- peak-month demand, and
- minimum-month demand.

Table 1–1 summarizes measurements of water use that are commonly used in the public water supply industry.

SELECTED SUPPLEMENTARY READINGS

Basic Ground-water Hydrology. 1983. Pub. WS 2220. Denver, Colo.: US Geological Survey.

Black, P.E. 1996. *Watershed Hydrology, 2nd ed.* Chelsea, Mich.: Sleeping Bear Press, Inc.

Driscoll, F.G. 1986. *Groundwater and Wells.* St. Paul, Minn.: Johnson Filtration Systems, Inc.

Dunne, T.D., and L.B. Leopold. 1978. Water in Environmental Planning. San Francisco, Calif.: W.H. Freeman and Company.

Ground Water and Surface Water; a Single Resource. 1998. US Geological Survey Circular 1139. Denver, Colo.: US Geological Survey.

Inside Rain, A Look at the National Atmospheric Deposition Program. 1999. National Atmospheric Deposition Program. Brochure 1999-01b (revised). Illinois State Water Survey. Available: http://nadp.sws.uiuc.edu.

Manual M32. Distribution Network Analysis for Water Utilities. 1989. Denver, Colo.: American Water Works Association.

Manual of Instruction for Water Treatment Plant Operators. 1989. Albany, N.Y.: New York State Department of Health.

Manual of Water Utility Operations, 8th ed. 1988. Austin, Tex.: Texas Water Utilities Association. Available: http://www.twua.org/publications.htm#wuo.

National Atmospheric Deposition Program 2000 Annual Summary. 2001. National Atmospheric Deposition Program. Data Report 2001-01. Illinois State Water Survey. Available: http://nadp.sws.uiuc.edu.

van der Leeden, F., F.L. Troise, and D.K. Todd. 1990. *The Water Encyclopedia, 2nd ed.* Chelsea, Mich.: Lewis Publishers.

TABLE 1–1 Common measurements of water use—US customary units

Term	Definition	How to Calculate	Units of Measure	Comments on Use
Volume	Amount of water that flows through a treatment plant	Read totalizer at beginning and end of period for which volume is to be determined, and subtract first reading from second.	Gallons, millions of gallons, cubic feet, acre-feet	One of the basic measurements of water use
Instantaneous flow rate	The flow rate at any instant	Read directly from circular flow chart or from indicator.	Gallons per minute (gpm), gallons per hour (gph), gallons per day (gpd), million gallons per day (mgd), cubic feet per second (ft^3/sec)	One of the basic measurements of water use
Daily flow	Amount of water passing through plant during a single day	Measure flow volume (gallons) for a single day.	gpd, mgd	Basis for calculating average daily flow and chemical designs
Average daily flow	Average of daily flows for a specified time period	Find sum of all daily flows for the period and divide by number of daily flows used.	gpd, mgd	Records of average daily flow rate are the basis for calculating most other measurements
Annual average daily flow	Average of average daily flows for a 12-month period	Average the average daily flows for all the days of the year, or divide total flow volume for the year by 365.	gpd, mgd	Used to predict need for system expansion

Table continued next page

TABLE 1-1 Common measurements of water use—US customary units (*continued*)

Term	Definition	How to Calculate	Units of Measure	Comments on Use
Peak-day demand	Greatest volume per day flowing through the plant for any day of the year	Look at records of daily flow rates for the year to find the peak day.	gpd, mgd	Determines system operation (plant output, storage) during heaviest load period—ranges from 1.5 to 3.5 times the average daily flow rate
Peak-hour demand	Greatest volume per hour flowing through the plant for any hour in the year	Determine from the chart recordings showing the continuous changes in flow rate.	gph	Determines required capacity of distribution system piping—ranges from 2.0 to 7.0 times the average hourly demand for the year
Minimum-day demand	Least volume per day flowing through the plant for any day of the year	Look at records of daily flow rates for the year to find the minimum day.	gpd, mgd	Determines possible plant shutdown periods—ranges from 0.5 to 0.8 times the average daily flow rate
Filtration rate	Rate at which water is flowing through a filter	Divide the flow rate per minute flowing through the filter by the surface area of the filter.	gpm/ft^2	Indicates the rate of flow through a filter, particularly to check that the design rate is not exceeded

Table continued next page

TABLE 1–1 Common measurements of water use—US customary units (*continued*)

Term	Definition	How to Calculate	Units of Measure	Comments on Use
Peak-month demand	Greatest volume passing through the plant during a calendar month	Look at records of daily flow volumes (determined from totalizer readings at the beginning and end of each month or from the sums of the daily flows for each month) to find peak month for the year.	Gallons, millions of gallons, billions of gallons	Determines possible plant storage needs—ranges from 1.1 to 1.5 times the average monthly flow volume for the year
Minimum-month demand	Least volume passing through the plant during a calendar month	Look at records of monthly flow volumes (determined as for peak-month demand) to find minimum month for the year.	Gallons, millions of gallons, billions of gallons	Best time of year for checking and repairing equipment—ranges from 0.75 to 0.90 times the average monthly flow volumes for a year
Minimum-hour demand	Least volume per hour flowing through the plant for any hour in the year	Determine from the chart recordings showing the continuous changes in flow rate.	gpm, gph	Ranges from 0.20 to 0.75 times the average hourly demand for a year

Groundwater Sources

Groundwater is an extremely important resource in North America. About 22 percent of all water withdrawn in the United States, including water used for agriculture, mining, and power, comes from groundwater. About 25 percent of this amount is used for public and domestic supply. Groundwater represents the principal source of potable water for about 40 percent of the country's population, with more than 97 percent of the rural population being served by wells (USGS Circular, 1998).

Groundwater sources can be relatively simple to develop and they often require little or no treatment before use. Small public water systems usually find groundwater the most economical source if suitable aquifers are available.

> *Groundwater represents the principal source of potable water for about 40 percent of the country's population.*

WATER WELL TERMINOLOGY

Wells are the most common means of accessing groundwater. This section describes the parts of a well and defines common terms associated with wells.

Parts of a Well

Although wells come in several different forms with varying components, the principal parts of a typical well are labeled in Figure 2–1. At the surface, all wells should have a sanitary seal, which prevents contamination from entering the well casing. The seal is generally a metal plate with a rubberized gasket around its perimeter that fits snugly into the top of

FIGURE 2-1 Parts of a typical well

the well casing. It has openings into the well for the discharge pipe, the pump power cable, and an air vent to let air into the casing as the water level drops. A sanitary seal for a small well having a submersible pump is illustrated in Figure 2–2.

The well casing is simply a liner placed in the borehole to prevent the walls from caving in. It is generally made of steel or plastic pipe and may not be necessary where the well extends into competent rock that has little risk of collapsing into

Air Vent

Discharge Line

Pump Power Cable

Sanitary Seal

Well Casing

FIGURE 2–2 Components of a sanitary seal

the well. In the case of competent rock, the casing is generally seated into the rock to prevent soil from falling into the well.

The space between the casing and borehole is filled with grout to help prevent water from traveling along the outside of the casing and to support the casing. In cases where the well penetrates several aquifers, the grout also keeps water from flowing between aquifers along the outside of the well.

Grout is a thin mixture of cement and water that may contain additives, which are used to give the grout desirable qualities. For example, bentonite may be added to help prevent the grout from cracking. Grout should be placed by pumping it through a pipe or hose (called a *tremie*) to the bottom of the casing. The tremie pipe is placed between the casing and the soil or rock. Pumping the grout from the bottom up ensures that no gaps or voids are left between the casing and soil or rock.

A well screen (intake screen) may be placed in a soil or highly fractured rock aquifer at intervals along the well where water intake is desired. The well screen prevents rock and soil from entering the well while letting in water. Often in a well that is screened in soil, sand is packed between the screen and the soil to fill the area and act as a rough screen to sand and sediment that would otherwise get into the well. In competent rock, water may enter the well mainly through fractures in the bedrock rather than through the pores of the rock. In this case, the fractured zones may be screened to prevent rock chips around the fracture from falling into the well.

The well slab is a concrete area placed around the casing of some wells to support pumping equipment and to help prevent surface water from contaminating the well water.

Well Terms

The hydraulic characteristics of a well that are important during well operation are

- static water level,
- pumping water level,
- drawdown,
- cone of depression,
- zone of influence,
- residual drawdown,
- well yield, and
- specific capacity.

Many of these characteristics are illustrated in Figure 2–3.

Static water level

The static water level in a well is the water surface in the well when no water is being taken from the aquifer. It is normally measured as the depth from the ground surface to the water surface and may be converted to elevation for comparison with information on other wells in the area. This is an important measurement because it is the basis for monitoring changes in the water table.

In some areas, the water table is just below the ground surface; usually, it is several feet below the surface. In other areas, there is no groundwater near the surface, and a well may not pass through any water until an aquifer is intercepted at hundreds or even thousands of feet below the surface.

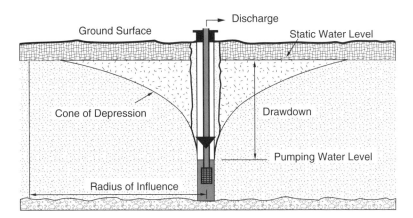

FIGURE 2–3 Hydraulic influence of a well on an aquifer

Pumping water level

When water is pumped out of a well, the water level usually drops below the level in the surrounding aquifer and eventually stabilizes at a lower level called the pumping level. The level will vary with pumping rate. The water intake or sub-merged pump must be located below this level. It is also preferred to limit the pumping rate so that this level is above the screened portion of the well or above water-bearing fractures in an open rock well to prevent water from continually cascading down the sides of the well.

Drawdown

The drop in water level between the static water level and the pumping water level is called the drawdown of the well.

Cone of depression

In unconfined aquifers, there is a flow of water in the aquifer from all directions toward the well during pumping. The free water surface in the aquifer then takes the shape of an inverted cone or curved funnel called the cone of depression. In a confined aquifer, the water pressure within the aquifer will also be much less at the well than at some distance from the well. A graph of the water pressure versus distance from the well will also have the shape of a curved funnel that is centered on the well.

Zone of influence

The zone affected by the drawdown extends out from the well a distance that depends on the porosity of the soil and other factors. The horizontal distance around a well that is drawn down is called the radius of influence, as shown in Figure 2–3. The length and depth of the radius define the zone of influence. If the aquifer is composed of material that transmits water easily, such as coarse sand or gravel, the cone may be almost flat and the zone of influence relatively small. If the material in the aquifer transmits water slowly, the cone will usually be quite steep and the zone of influence large.

If possible, wells should be situated far enough apart that their zones of influence do not overlap. The effect on the cones of depression of two wells located close together is illustrated in Figure 2–4. Pumping a single well reduces the water level in the other well, and pumping both simultaneously creates an undesirable interference in the drawdown profiles.

Residual drawdown

After pumping is stopped, the water level in a well will rise toward the static water level. If the water level does not quite reach the original level, the distance it falls short is called the residual drawdown.

FIGURE 2–4 Overlapping cones of depression of two wells

Well yield

Well yield is the rate of water withdrawal that a well can supply over a long period of time. The yield of small wells is usually measured in gallons per minute (liters per minute) or gallons per hour (liters per hour). For large wells, it may be measured in cubic feet per second (cubic meters per second).

When the pumpage from an aquifer continually exceeds the water recharge to the aquifer, more water is being taken from the aquifer than is being placed back into it. The drawdown will gradually extend to greater depths and the safe well yield will be reduced. If, under prolonged pumping, the drawdown extends to below the pump suction, the pump will begin to suck air. This can damage the pump, so it must be avoided by limiting the pumping rate within the well.

Other options for avoiding pump damage by sucking in air include lowering the pump setting (depth of the pump) and operating the well for only short periods of time. This will limit the drawdown and allow the well to "rest" while the water level recovers before the pump is operated again.

Specific capacity

One of the most important concepts in well operation and testing is specific capacity. It is a measure of well yield per unit of drawdown, or

$$\text{specific capacity} = \text{well yield} \div \text{drawdown}$$

For example, if the well yield is 200 gpm and the drawdown is measured to be 25 ft, the specific capacity is

$$200 \div 25 = \text{specific capacity}$$
$$\text{specific capacity} = 8 \text{ gpm per 1 ft of drawdown}$$

The calculation is simple and should be made frequently in the monitoring of well operation. A sudden drop in specific capacity indicates trouble such as pump wear, screen plugging, or other problems that can be serious. These problems should be identified and corrected as soon as possible.

WELL LOCATION

A well should be located to produce the maximum yield possible while still being protected as much as possible from contamination. A number of methods can be used to determine likely locations for a new well installation.

Existing Data

When a new well is to be constructed, the first places to look for information are the state and federal geological or water resources agencies. In most states, data from previous well logs have been used to draw maps of the geology of various regions and to define water-bearing layers. The agencies should also be of assistance in identifying the productivity of aquifers in the region and determining which of them is capable of providing flow to additional wells.

They will probably also have information on water quality, including data on hardness, iron and manganese, sulfur, nitrate, radionuclides, and other water characteristics that might be of concern. The state agency may also be able to provide some information on the possibility of contamination of the aquifer from organic chemicals.

The owners of surrounding public and private wells are another source of information. If there is more than one aquifer in the area, it is important that the information obtained applies only to wells in the aquifer being considered for the new well. Although there are often some differences in water quality within an aquifer, the information from existing wells gives a fair idea of what can be expected in a new well.

Local well-drilling contractors are the third source of information that should be used. They usually have extensive practical information on where wells can be developed and on the quantity and quality of water that will be obtained.

A hydrogeologist is one who understands both the geologic and groundwater environment and is often familiar with local or state regulations regarding the permitting of water supply wells. A local, licensed hydrogeologist can provide invaluable help in determining the most likely location to drill a well that suits the needs of the owner. This is especially true in areas where water is scarce or no large aquifers exist.

Likely Locations

As one might expect, groundwater is likely to be present in larger quantities under valleys than under hills. Valley soils containing permeable material washed down from mountains are usually productive aquifers. In some areas of the country, the only groundwater of usable quality is found in river valleys. Also, the bedrock underlying valleys is often fractured and water-bearing. Coastal terraces as well as coastal and river plains may also have good aquifers.

Any evidence of surface water, such as streams, springs, seeps, swamps, or lakes, is a good indicator that there is groundwater present, though not necessarily in usable quantities. Sometimes vegetation will show the location of groundwater; an unusually thick overgrowth may indicate shallow groundwater.

Exploration

After all existing data and likely locations have been examined, there still may not be enough information to risk spending a large amount of money on a full-size well. It is then advisable to conduct an underground exploration to provide additional information on geologic formations and aquifers. Some of the more common methods include using geophysical exploration, drilling test wells, and using computer modeling.

Geophysical exploration

If there is inadequate information on groundwater in an area, one possible next step in exploration is to employ a professional firm to perform a geophysical survey. The science of geophysics uses indirect means to characterize the subsurface and is often a cost-effective way to unravel the larger geologic picture and to find specific objects in the subsurface. Understanding the overall geologic picture will often help in understanding where the best location to drill a well might be. Specific targets that geophysicists might use to locate a well include water-bearing faults and fracture zones in the bedrock and the lateral and vertical extent of specific aquifers. A professional geophysicist, in coordination with a hydrogeologist, should determine the most appropriate geophysical technique for the specified purpose and location. However, several common techniques are used including seismic and resistivity methods.

Seismic methods measure the speed at which a sound wave travels through the earth. The velocities can be correlated to geologic formations that may contain groundwater. A small charge of dynamite is discharged at the bottom of a drilled shot hole. The time required for the sound waves to pass through the ground and reach vibration sensors (called geophones) placed at spaced distances at the surface is measured (Figure 2–5). The time recorded at the various locations can be used to determine where water-bearing formations might be located. Resistivity methods measure the ground's electrical resistance with depth into the ground. In general, the lower the electrical resistance, the greater the probability that water is present. Both tests can be conducted on the ground surface, without the need to drill test holes.

Test wells

If it appears likely that water is present, exploration holes can be drilled in key locations. Samples of the material removed as drilling progresses on each hole should be kept. The holes may then be logged electrically or by using gamma rays to help define water-bearing formations. Electric logging measures the change in the earth's resistance to an electrical current as the depth increases. Gamma-ray logging measures how controlled radiation penetrates the earth. Information from

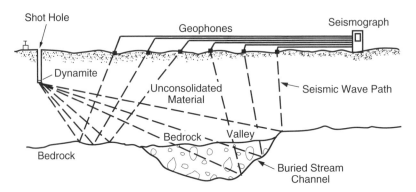

FIGURE 2–5 Application of the seismic refraction method for reconnaissance mapping

the logs is correlated with the samples removed during the drilling to identify the various formations below the surface.

Computer modeling

Hydrologists interested in evaluating the many complex stresses and effects on an aquifer system can now use computer programs to perform studies that were not previously possible with manual calculations (Figure 2–6). This type of analysis might be necessary, for example, in areas where several wells are stressing the aquifer to determine an allowable maximum yield. Computer analyses using available information on aquifer recharge and withdrawals can also be used to rapidly forecast the most appropriate locations of additional wells, the effects of contamination sources on the aquifer, and many other factors. At present, computer models are most widely used by government agencies to develop area and regional plans for groundwater use.

Sources of Groundwater Contamination

New wells must be located a safe distance from sources of potential contamination. Contamination is usually considered to be the result of human activities near or at the surface, such as a leaking storage tank. However, contamination may also be the result of overpumping, as in the case of salt-water intrusion or surface water capture, or the result of the naturally occurring substances, such as radon, asbestos, or iron. Typically, a minimum radial distance from the top of the well (wellhead protection area) is regulated by local and state environmental agencies. The regulations generally limit the type and extent of activities that can be conducted within the wellhead protection area.

FIGURE 2–6 A computer being used to model groundwater conditions

Existing wells sometimes become contaminated because of new contamination sources or sources that were not anticipated when the well was installed. Potential sources of groundwater contamination are listed in Table 2–1.

These contaminants may be naturally occurring or synthetic and may be located on or below the ground surface. If the contaminants were injected into the soil, it could have been done through ignorance, by accident, or by intentional illegal disposal. Contaminants can be carried into an aquifer along with percolating surface water and can travel considerable distances under certain conditions.

Problems caused by contaminants can include disagreeable tastes and odors, presence of disease-causing organisms, and levels of chemical contaminants above recommended health-related limits for drinking water. Generally, state environmental agencies provide maximum contaminant levels, which govern the usage of water containing contaminants.

Because of differences in soil permeability, the depth of soil, and types of underlying materials, as well as the varying rates and directions of groundwater movement, there is no set safe distance that applies to all wells. Some chemical contaminants have been tracked more than 0.5 mi (0.8 km) from their source.

TABLE 2–1 Potential sources of groundwater contamination

Source	Possible Major Contaminants
Landfills	
Municipal	Heavy metals, chloride, sodium, calcium
Industrial	Wide variety of organic and inorganic constituents
Hazardous-waste disposal sites	Wide variety of inorganic constituents (particularly heavy metals such as hexavalent chromium) and organic compounds (pesticides, solvents, polychlorinated biphenyls)
Liquid waste storage ponds (lagoons, leaching ponds, and evaporation basins)	Heavy metals, solvents, and brines
Septic tanks and leach fields	Organic compounds (solvents), nitrates, sulfates, sodium, and microbiological contaminants
Deep-well waste injection	Variety of organic and inorganic compounds
Agricultural activities	Nitrates, herbicides, and pesticides
Land application of wastewater and sludges	Heavy metals, organic compounds, inorganic compounds, and microbiological contaminants
Infiltration of urban runoff	Inorganic compounds, heavy metals, and petroleum products
Deicing activities (control of snow and ice on roads)	Chlorides, sodium, and calcium
Radioactive wastes	Radioactivity from strontium, tritium, and other radionuclides
Improperly abandoned wells and exploration holes	Variety of organic, inorganic, and microbiological contaminants from surface runoff and other contaminated aquifers

Source:　Basics of Well Construction Operator's Guide

When siting a new well, one must keep in mind that when the well is put into operation, the direction of groundwater flow could change. As illustrated in Figure 2–7, water flow in an aquifer that appears to be coming from a direction with no contamination can actually be reversed by a new well's zone of influence. This illustrates the need for continual sampling and analysis of public supply water sources for contamination.

Site Selection

Eventually, all available data are combined for study and the test site is selected. Unfortunately, the best site from a geological standpoint may not always be available for installation of a well. In a residential community, for instance, the decision of where to site a new well must also be based on where land can be acquired and where the construction of a well will be aesthetically acceptable to residents.

FIGURE 2–7 Reversal of flow in an aquifer due to well drawdown

33

TYPES OF WELLS

Wells are holes sunk into the earth to obtain water from an aquifer. The type of construction generally classifies them as follows:

- dug wells,
- bored wells,
- driven wells,
- jetted wells, and
- drilled wells.

Dug Wells

A dug well can furnish large quantities of water from shallow groundwater sources. Dug wells are not common because of the cost to install them and the potential for contamination of the shallow aquifers and wells. Small-diameter wells are generally constructed manually with pick and shovel; larger wells are constructed with machinery such as a clamshell bucket if suitable soil conditions are encountered. Figure 2–8 illustrates a typical dug-well installation.

If the exposed soil will stand without support, it may not be necessary to line the excavation until the water table is reached. Precast or cast-in-place concrete liners, commonly called curbs, are used to seal the shaft from groundwater contamination. The liners in contact with the water-bearing layers are perforated to allow water to enter. If the aquifer is sandy material, a layer of gravel is placed around the curb to act as a sand barrier.

Yield from a dug well increases with an increase in diameter, but the increase is not directly proportional. Dug wells serving a public water system may be 8 to 30 ft (2 to 9 m) in diameter and from 20 to 40 ft (6 to 12 m) deep.

Most dug wells do not penetrate much below the water table because of the difficulty of excavating in the saturated soil. For this reason, a dug well may fail if the water level recedes during times of drought or if there is unusually heavy pumpage from the well.

The opening of a dug well has a large surface area, making protection from surface contamination difficult. For that reason, state regulatory agencies usually classify these wells as being vulnerable to contamination, and the wells must be treated as a surface water source. Disinfection and possibly filtration treatment will be required if the water source is to be used by a public water system.

Bored Wells

Wells can be constructed quickly by boring if the soil types are suitable. The soil must be soft enough for an auger to penetrate yet firm enough so it will not cave

FIGURE 2–8 Construction of a dug well

in before a liner can be installed. The most suitable formations for bored wells are glacial till and alluvial valley deposits.

The well is constructed by driving an auger into the earth. Bored wells are limited to approximately 3 ft (1 m) in diameter and depths of 25 to 60 ft (8 to 18 m) under suitable conditions. As the auger penetrates, extensions are added to the drive shaft. A casing is forced into the hole as material is removed until the water-bearing strata are reached. Installing well screens or a perforated casing in the water-bearing sand and gravel layer completes the well.

Cement grout is used to surround the casing to prevent entrance of surface water, which could cause contamination. Bored wells are not frequently used for public water supplies.

Driven Wells

Driven wells are simple to install; however, they are practical only when the water-bearing soils are relatively close to the surface and no boulders or bedrock exist in the soil between the surface and the aquifer. These wells consist of a pointed well screen, called a drive point, and lengths of pipe attached to the point. The point has a steel tip that enables it to be pounded through some gravel or hardpan (a hard layer of cemented soil near the ground surface) to the water-bearing soil (Figure 2–9).

Galvanized
Steel Alloy or
Stainless-Steel
Construction
Throughout

**Continuous
Slot Type**

**Brass Jacket
Type**

**Brass Tube
Type**

Source: Manual of Individual Water Supply Systems *(1982).*

FIGURE 2–9 Different types of driven-well points

The diameter of the well pipe varies from as small as 1 in. (32 mm) up to 4 in. (107 mm). The maximum depth that can be achieved is generally 30 to 40 ft (9 to 12 m). This well type is not generally used for public water supply because of the potential for environmental contamination of shallow aquifers and because of their relatively small diameter—a single well cannot produce the quantity of water generally needed for public supply. However, a battery of points may be used for greater production, with several wells connected by a common header to a suction-type pump. A suction pump can be used only when the static water level is no deeper than about 15 ft (5 m).

A smaller diameter pilot hole is usually drilled or driven before driving the well to make installation easier and help prevent damage of the well casing. This casing of durable pipe can be pounded into the earth or placed in a bored hole. The casing prevents water contamination if there should be leaky joints in the well pipe.

After the outer casing is in place, the inner casing with a perforated well point is inserted. The drive point is then driven into the water-bearing formation.

Jetted Wells

The equipment used to construct jetted wells consists of a jetting pipe, which is equipped with a cutting knife on the bottom. Water is pumped down the pipe and out of the drill bit against the bottom of the hole. The high-pressure water jet at the bottom of the pipe, in coordination with the cutting knife, loosens and removes the soil beneath the pipe and allows the pipe to advance downward.

The casing is usually sunk as the drilling progresses, until it passes through the water-bearing formation. The well screen connected to a smaller diameter pipe is then lowered into the casing, and the outer casing is withdrawn to expose the screen to the formation. These wells are generally suited to sandy soils and cannot be constructed by jetting through clay or hardpan or where there are boulders in the soil.

Drilled Wells

Drilled wells are the most commonly used well type for public water supplies because they can be installed in almost any situation. They can be constructed to extreme depths with small or large well diameters (up to 4 ft [1.5 m] or possibly larger). They are also the most common type of well drilled for oil extraction.

A drilled well is constructed using a drilling rig and casing. The rig makes the hole and casing is placed in the hole to prevent the walls from collapsing. Screens are installed when water-bearing formations are encountered at one or more levels.

The following are the more commonly used methods of drilling water supply wells:

- cable tool method,
- rotary hydraulic method,
- reverse-circulation rotary method,
- California method,
- rotary air method, and
- down-the-hole hammer method.

Cable tool method

The percussion drilling method, commonly referred to as the cable tool method, has been used extensively for wells of all sizes and depths but has waned in popularity in the past 20 years due to faster and easier methods. There are many commercial varieties of cable tool rigs. The operating principle for all varieties is the same. They use a bit at the end of a cable that is repeatedly raised and dropped to fracture the soil material. The drilling tool has a club-like chisel edge that breaks the formation into small fragments. The reciprocating motion of the drilling tool mixes the loosened material into a sludge-like substance.

In each run of the drill, a depth of 3 to 6 ft (1 to 2 m) of the hole is drilled. The drill is then pulled from the hole, and a bailer is used to remove the sludge. The bailer consists of a 10- to 25-ft (3- to 8-m) long section of casing that is slightly smaller in diameter than the drilled hole and has a check valve in the bottom. A casing is forced into the hole as soon as it is necessary to prevent a cave-in of the walls.

As the drill operates, an operator continually adjusts the length of stroke and rapidity of blows based on experience and on the feel of the vibrations. The operator can also generally distinguish the hardness of the formation being drilled by the vibrations in the cable and can sense the passing of the drill from one formation to another. Samples of the cuttings are also periodically taken to check on the type of formation being penetrated.

After drilling the well to the maximum desired depth, a screen is lowered inside the casing and held in place while the casing is pulled back to expose the screen (Figure 2–10). The top of the screen is then sealed against the casing by expanding a packer of neoprene rubber or lead. When a well reaches consolidated rock, normal practice is to "seat" the casing firmly in the top of the rock and drill an open hole to the depth required to obtain the needed yield (Figure 2–11).

FIGURE 2-10 Exposed well screen

Rotary hydraulic method

In the rotary method of well drilling, the hole is made by spinning a cylinder-shaped bit on the bottom of multiple sections of drill pipe. The speed of rotation can be varied to achieve the best cutting effectiveness for different formations.

Drilling fluid (typically a thin slurry of clay and water, also called drilling mud) is pumped down to the bit (Figure 2–12). The fluid flows out through holes in the bit, picks up loosened material, and carries it up the borehole to the surface. The circulating fluid also helps to cool the bit and keep the hole open during drilling.

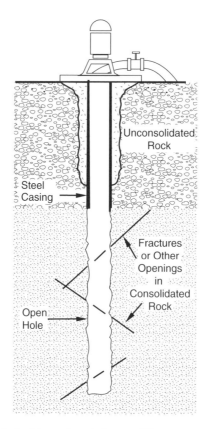

FIGURE 2-11 Casing seated at top of rock layer with an open hole underneath

The fluid that flows to the surface overflows from the well and is routed by a ditch into a settling pit or tub where the cuttings settle out. The fluid can then be reused.

Clay is usually added to the drilling fluid. It will adhere to the sides of the hole and, together with the pressure exerted by the drilling fluid, it prevents a cave-in of the formation material. In some cases, native clay can be used; otherwise, prepared materials such as bentonite (a commercially available, highly expansive clay) or a special powdered material is used. The drilling fluid is prepared in a pit near the drilling operation prior to being pumped into the well and can be varied depending upon the material that is being drilled through.

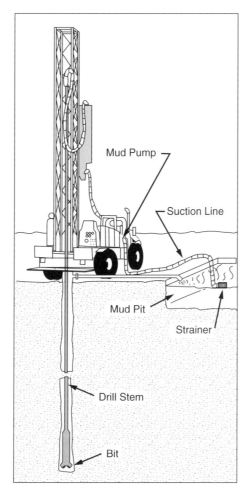

FIGURE 2–12 Circulation of drilling fluid in a direct rotary drilling rig

Reverse-circulation rotary method

The reverse-circulation rotary method of drilling differs from the regular rotary method in that the drilling fluid is circulated in the opposite direction. The advantage of this method is that generally water is used as the drilling fluid and the method can be used where drilling additives are undesirable. This method is also particularly well suited for constructing gravel-packed wells, because the drilling fluid mixture used in the regular rotary method tends to plug the walls of the well.

Drilling fluid is forced down through the borehole and returns to the surface in the hollow drill pipe, carrying the cuttings with it. A pump with a capacity of 500 gpm (1,900 L/min) or more is required to keep the fluid moving at high velocity. If an abundant freshwater supply is available, the discharge can be diverted to waste and not recycled. Otherwise, the cuttings are allowed to settle in a large pit and the fluid is recirculated.

Both rotary methods can drill holes up to 5 ft (1.5 m) in diameter, and the drilling is usually faster than cable tool drilling.

California method

The stovepipe, or California, method was developed primarily for sinking wells in unconsolidated material such as alternating strata of clay, sand, and gravel. The process is similar to the cable tool method except that a special bucket is used as both bit and bailer. Each time the bit is dropped, some of the cuttings are trapped in the bailer. When the bailer is filled, it is raised to the surface and emptied.

The process also uses short lengths of sheet metal for casing. The casing is forced down by hydraulic jacks or driven by means of cable tools. After the casing is in place, it is perforated in place using special tools.

Rotary air method

The rotary air method of drilling is similar to the rotary hydraulic method except that the drilling fluid is air rather than a mixture of water and clay. The method is suitable only for drilling in consolidated rock. Most large drill rigs are equipped for both air and hydraulic drilling so that the method may be changed as varying strata are encountered.

Down-the-hole hammer method

A method frequently chosen to drill wells into rock uses a pneumatic hammer unit that is attached to the end of the drill pipe. The hammer is operated by compressed air. The air also cleans the cuttings away from the bit and carries them to the surface. For most types of rock, this is the fastest drilling method available.

The drilling rig for this method must be furnished with a very large air compressor. Most standard rigs use 750 to 1,050 ft^3/min (0.35 to 0.49 m^3/sec) of air at a pressure of 250 psi (1,700 kPa). Some rigs are also capable of operating at 350 psi (2,400 kPa), which will advance the drill twice as fast as a standard rig. A drilling rig of this type is illustrated in Figure 2–13.

Courtesy of Ingersoll-Rand Company

FIGURE 2–13 A modern drilling rig

Special Types of Wells

Unlike the previously described wells, there are several other types that are not named according to the method of construction. These types include

- radial wells,
- gravel-wall wells, and
- bedrock wells.

Radial wells

Radial wells are commonly used near the shore of a lake or near a river to obtain a large amount of relatively good-quality water from adjacent sand or gravel beds. Radial wells are also used in place of multiple vertical wells to obtain water from a relatively shallow aquifer or to obtain water from a surface body while the soil underneath a river or lake is used as a filter. A radial well can be described as a dug well that has horizontal wells projecting outward from the bottom of the vertical central well (Figure 2–14). The central well, or caisson, serves as the water collector for the water produced by the horizontal screened wells.

Construction begins by sinking the central caisson, which is generally 15 to 20 ft (5 to 6 m) in diameter. The caisson is made by stacking poured-in-place reinforced concrete rings, each about 8 to 10 ft (2 to 3 m) high. The first section is formed with a cutting edge to facilitate the caisson's settling within the excavation. As soil is excavated from within the caisson, the concrete ring sinks into place. Additional sections are then added and the excavation progresses. When the desired depth is reached, a concrete plug is poured to make a floor.

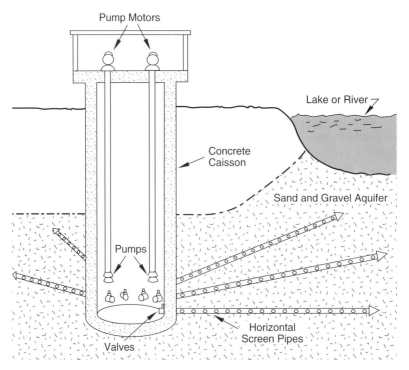

FIGURE 2–14 Details of a radial well

Horizontal wells are then constructed through wall sleeves near the bottom of the water-bearing strata. The laterals may be constructed of slotted or perforated pipe or they may have conventional well screens. Each horizontal well is constructed with a gate valve located inside the caisson for subsequent dewatering or to discontinue use of individual collector wells. A superstructure is then erected on top of the caisson to house pumps, piping, and controls.

Gravel-wall wells

Gravel-wall wells are also commonly called gravel-packed wells. They are best used in formations composed of fine-grained soils having uniform grain size. As illustrated in Figure 2–15, a bed of gravel is installed around the screen, which in effect gives greater surface area for the infiltration of water into the well, while effectively blocking the entrance of sand.

The most common construction method is to install a large-diameter casing into the water-bearing strata and then lower a small casing with a well screen into the hole. The area around the screen is then filled with gravel as the outer casing is withdrawn corresponding to the length of the screen. The gravel used must be clean, washed, and composed of well-rounded particles that are four to five times larger than the median size of the surrounding natural material. The size and gradation of the gravel are critical in effectively blocking the entrance of fine sand.

Bedrock wells

Bedrock wells are drilled into the underlying bedrock. Water flows to the well through fractures in the bedrock rather than from a saturated layer.

WELL CONSTRUCTION PROCEDURES

Wells can be constructed using a number of different procedures. The principal differences in the method used are how deep the well must be and whether the material that must be penetrated is gravel, clay, or rock. After a well has been constructed, it is usually necessary to specially treat the well to obtain optimum productivity and water quality. The last step in well construction is to run pumping tests to confirm the well's capacity.

Well Components

The components that are common to most wells are

- well casings,
- well screens, and
- grouting.

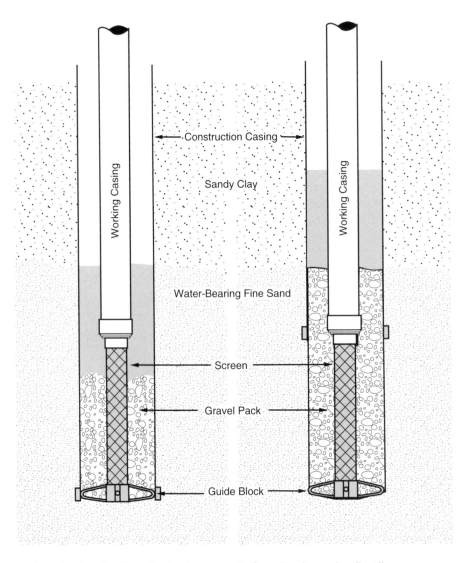

A. Gravel-wall well with casing in place   **B. Completed gravel-wall well**

FIGURE 2–15 Gravel-wall well construction

Well casings

The well casing is a lining for the drilled hole that maintains the stability of the open hole from the land surface to the water-bearing formation. Casing also prevents surface water from contaminating the water being drawn from the well.

Materials commonly used for well casings include wrought iron, alloyed or unalloyed steel, ingot iron, fiberglass, and plastic. The principal factors in determining the suitability of a casing material are the stress that will be placed on the casing during the installation and the corrosiveness of the water and soil that will be in contact with the casing.

Many weights of steel and wrought iron casing material are available for use under varying conditions. Lightweight materials are often used for test wells and temporary wells.

When a well is being drilled by the cable tool method, the casing is driven as soon as it becomes necessary to prevent the walls of the well from caving in. A drive shoe of hardened steel is attached to the lower end of the pipe, and a drive head is attached to the top of the pipe to withstand the hard blows of driving the casing into the ground. As the drilling progresses, the casing is continually pounded by the action of the drilling equipment.

Wells constructed using rotary methods are not usually cased until the well hole has been completed. A casing diameter smaller than the hole is used so that the casing does not have to be driven.

If additional protection from corrosion and surface water pollution is required, an outer casing is first installed, an inner casing is lowered into place, and the space between them is filled with cement grout. The outer casing may be left in place or it may be withdrawn as the grout is added.

Well screens

Wells completed in unconsolidated formations, such as sand and gravel, are usually equipped with screens (Figure 2–16). A properly sized screen will allow the maximum amount of water from the aquifer to enter the well with a minimum of resistance, while blocking formation materials from passing into the well. Well screens are made from a variety of materials, including plastic, mild steel, red brass, bronze, and stainless steel. Types of well screens include sawn or slotted, wound, and bridged and louvered. The type of screen and material used depends on the type of soil, corrosivity of the water, cleaning and redevelopment methods, and other factors.

The size of a screen, or the slot number, is usually expressed in thousandths of an inch or millimeters. The slot size is usually selected to permit some of the formation material to pass through it, depending on the uniformity of the grains. During development of the well, the fines pass through the screen while larger

FIGURE 2–16 Properly designed well screen

particles are held back, forming a graded natural-gravel barrier around the screen (Figure 2–17). A gravel pack is often placed between the screen and the formation to help stabilize the formation materials.

The open area of the screen after the well has been developed must be carefully estimated because up to 50 percent of the screen slots may be plugged by formation particles. After the slot size has been determined, either the screen length or diameter must be adjusted to provide the total required screen opening.

Information and specifications for screen selection are furnished in AWWA A100, *Standard for Water Wells* (latest edition).

Grouting

Wells are cemented, or grouted, in order to

- seal the well from possible surface water pollution;
- seal out water from water-bearing strata that have unsatisfactory quality;

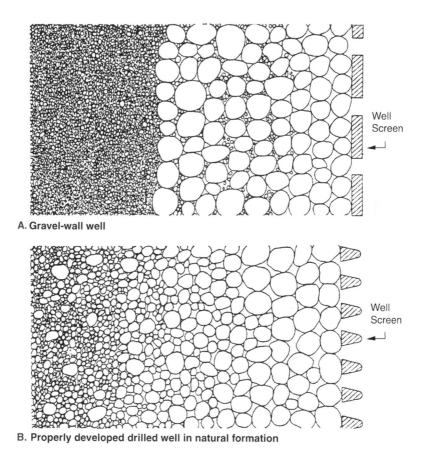

A. Gravel-wall well

B. Properly developed drilled well in natural formation

FIGURE 2–17 Coarse material used to hold fine sand away from a well screen

- protect the casing against exterior corrosion; and
- restrain unstable soil and rock formations.

When a well is drilled, an annular space is left between the casing and the formation material. This space must be sealed in order to prevent contaminants from entering, either from the land surface or from formations with crevices connected with the surface (Figure 2–18). In formations that typically cave in, such as sand, the cavity will tend to seal itself eventually; in stable formations, such as solid rock, the cavity may remain indefinitely if not filled.

When corrosion of the casing is likely, a well is usually drilled larger than the casing so that the extra space can be filled with grout. Grout is typically either cement or bentonite. Portland-cement grout is usually mixed in a ratio of about one bag of cement to 5.5 gal (21 L) of clean water. Special additives are often used to accelerate or retard the time of setting and provide other special properties to the grout. In some areas, bentonite clay is used instead of cement to fill the voids around the casing.

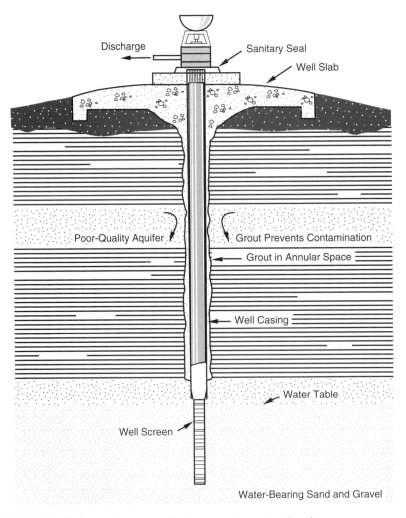

FIGURE 2–18 Sealed annular space that prevents contamination

The grout must be placed in the annular space, starting at the bottom and progressing upward so that no gaps or voids exist in the seal. Different methods may be used to place the grout depending on the size of the annular space, including a dump-bailer, water-pressure driving, pumping, or a tremie pour. Grout must be placed in compliance with state regulations.

Well Development

After a well is constructed, various techniques are used to develop the well—that is, to allow the well to produce the best-quality water at the highest rate from the aquifer. The method used is dependent on many different factors and is usually selected by the well construction contractor. Methods commonly used include

- high-rate pumping,
- surging,
- increased-rate pumping and surging,
- use of explosives,
- high-velocity jetting,
- chemical agents,
- pressure acidizing, or
- hydraulic fracturing ("fracking").

High-rate pumping

When a well draws water from a rock aquifer where no screen is used, development usually involves simply pumping the well at a rate higher than the normal production rate. This is done to flush out the casing and surrounding aquifer of fine material.

Surging

Surging generally employs a plunger, or surge block, on a tool string, which is moved up and down in the well casing (Figure 2–19). This creates flow reversals in the well face that dislodge the fine material and allow it to fall to the bottom of the well. The fines can then be removed with a bailer. Various types of surge blocks are used.

Surging is also achieved by use of compressed air. A seal is made at the top of the casing so that applied air pressure will drive the water in the well back through the screen or exposed walls of the well. A jet of compressed air is then used to raise fine material that has been freed up to the surface for removal. When this system is used, care must be taken not to drive air into the formation because it may collect in pockets that will reduce the aquifer production.

A. Details of a typical surge block

B. Surge block being used to develop a well by
pulling silt and fine sand through the screen

FIGURE 2-19 Surge block schematics

Increased-rate pumping and surging

Increasing the pumping rate in combination with surging is effective in developing wells in unconsolidated limestone. As much of the drilling fluid as possible is first removed from the well and, as the water clears, gentle surging assists in development. Pumping rates are gradually increased in steps to develop the well fully.

Use of explosives

Explosives may be used in well development to fracture massive rock formations and create fractures that allow water to flow. Heavy charges are set off in the well bore at predetermined points to radiate fractures outward from the bore. Another technique is to shoot dynamite in the most permeable portions of a formation to clear drilling mud or other materials that are plugging the bore face. Another method is to set off very light charges in a series of explosions to produce vibrations that agitate the materials surrounding the bore. With any of these explosive methods, the loosened material must be removed from the well, usually by bailing.

High-velocity jetting

Hydraulic jetting involves high-pressure pumping of clean water against the sides of the well. When the force strikes the formation, it breaks down dense compacted materials and mud left from rotary drilling. The jets are rotated at intervals of from 6 to 12 in. (150 to 305 mm) throughout the water-entry area of the well. The well is simultaneously pumped out at a rate higher than the rate at which jet water is being introduced.

Chemical agents

It has been found that chemical additives frequently enhance the effectiveness of various development methods. For instance, wetting agents used with hexametaphosphates are particularly useful in increasing the effectiveness of jetting. Acids may also be used where there are iron or carbonate deposits that must be dispersed.

Hydraulic fracturing

Hydraulic fracturing is a process in which a fluid is forced into the well under pressure great enough to open the separations between strata and along existing fractures. Gelling agents and selected sand are added to the fluid to hold the fractures open after pressure is removed. This process can be used only in rock aquifers, and the well casing must be firmly sealed and anchored in place.

Pumping Tests

After a well is developed and the quality of water produced is satisfactory, pumping tests are performed. These practical tests are intended to confirm that the well will produce at its design capacity. Most water supply well contracts require a guaranteed yield and may also stipulate that a certain level of well efficiency be reached. Contracts also usually specify the duration of the drawdown test that must be conducted to demonstrate that the yield requirement is met.

Many well acceptance tests are conducted with a temporary pump installed, usually powered by a gasoline or diesel engine. The test period for public water supply wells is generally at least 24 hours for a confined aquifer and 72 hours for an unconfined aquifer.

A means of measuring the flow rate of the pumped water must be provided. A commercial water meter, an orifice or weir, or periodic checking of the time required to fill a container of known volume are all methods of measuring flow rate. The pumping rate must be held constant during the test period and the depth to the water level in the well must periodically be measured. Drawdown is usually measured frequently (often at 1-minute intervals) during the first hour or so of the test and is then measured at gradually longer intervals (often up to 10-minute intervals) as the test period progresses.

Sanitary Considerations

Whenever possible, wells should be developed from formations deep enough to protect the water from surface contamination. Where a shallow groundwater source must be used, surface water contamination can be reduced if an impervious surface is created over the ground surface surrounding the well. One method is to place a 2-ft (0.6-m) layer of clay having a radius of about 50 ft (15 m) around the well. Filling the space between the casing and the hole with cement grout prevents contamination of wells by surface water flowing along the exterior of the casing. A concrete cap or platform should then be put in place around the well. The construction methods for wells are detailed by state regulatory agencies and, in some cases, by local jurisdiction as well. The well driller must follow the requirements, and the installation must be approved before the well is certified for use.

It is almost impossible to completely avoid contamination of the soil, tools, aquifer, casing, and screen during construction, so the water from the well, even after development, is likely to be contaminated. Extended pumping will usually rid the well of contamination, but disinfection with a chlorine solution is often quicker and more desirable.

A well is typically disinfected by the addition of sufficient chlorine to give a concentration of 50 mg/L. The pump can then be started and stopped to surge the disinfectant into and out of the aquifer, throughout the length of the well, and through the pump components. Gravel packing is difficult to disinfect by this procedure, so powdered or tablet calcium hypochlorite is usually added when the gravel is being placed.

For more details and specific procedures, refer to AWWA C654, *Standard for Disinfection of Wells* (latest edition).

AQUIFER PERFORMANCE

Aquifer performance is vital to the sustained performance of a well. Aquifer parameters also define how pumping in one well will affect other wells. These parameters are generally obtained via the pumping tests performed after well construction is complete. To measure changes in an aquifer during the pumping tests, small-diameter test wells, called observation wells, are installed. There is no set number of observation wells that should be used. One well positioned near an operating well will sometimes be sufficient, but several may be required under different circumstances.

Aquifer Evaluation

Observation wells are located carefully on a map. The distances measured between the well being tested and the observation wells, and between the observation wells themselves, are also recorded. The water level in each observation well is periodically measured relative to an elevation reference point, or benchmark.

One method of measuring the water depth in a test well is to use a steel tape graduated in tenths and hundredths of a foot (or metric units), with a weight attached (Figure 2–20A). The tape is chalked and lowered into the well until the weight reaches the bottom. When the tape is withdrawn, the water depth is indicated by the wetted position on the tape. Electronic depth-measuring devices are also available. They include a probe that is lowered into the well to activate a signal when water is contacted (Figure 2–20B).

Another way of measuring water depth, effectively used for many years for fixed installations, is the air-pressure tube method (Figure 2–20c). A small-diameter tube is suspended in the well beneath the water level, and the exact distance from the bottom of the tube to the ground surface is known. The top of the tube is fitted with a pressure gauge and a source of compressed air. Determining the water depth involves forcing air into the tube until it bubbles from the submerged end of the tube. The pressure gauge is then read, and the submerged length of tube can be calculated from the pressure required to displace the column of water in the tube. The calculation method is detailed in *Basic Science Concepts and Applications*, part of this series.

A. Chalked steel tape

B. Electronic measurement

C. Air-pressure tube method

FIGURE 2–20 Methods of measuring water level depth in wells

Evaluating Performance

Aquifer performance can be evaluated by the following three methods:

- drawdown method,
- recovery method, or
- specific-capacity method.

In the drawdown method, the production well is pumped and water levels are periodically observed in two or more observation wells. The data are plotted and can be analyzed by various methods to relate drawdown in feet (or meters) to time measured in hours or days at a specific pump rate.

The recovery method involves measuring the change in water level in an observation well after the pumping has been stopped.

The specific-capacity method involves a relatively short test. As discussed earlier, specific capacity is the well yield per unit of drawdown. It does not indicate aquifer performance as completely as the other tests. However, it is especially valuable in evaluating well production after a period of time and in making comparisons with the data from when the well was new.

WELL OPERATION AND MAINTENANCE

When a well is in service, it is important to keep records that will indicate any changes that might predict future problems. The following tests should be conducted and data recorded for each well:

- static water level after the pump has been idle for a period of time,
- pumping water level,
- drawdown,
- well production,
- well yield,
- time required for recovery after pumping, and
- specific capacity.

Conditions for the above tests should be the same each month so that direct comparisons can be made.

Regular maintenance of all the structures, equipment, and accessories is important to provide long-term, trouble-free service. Wells can fail if the casing or screen collapses or corrodes through. Probably the most common well operational problem is plugging of the screen. The causes can be mechanical, chemical, or bacteriological in nature. It is usually best to get professional assistance in correcting the problem. If the screen is accidentally damaged, repair can be extremely expensive or the entire well may have to be replaced.

Bacteriological samples should periodically be collected directly from each well and tested. If there are indications of contamination, periodic disinfection of a well may be necessary to prevent growth of nuisance bacteria that can lead to production problems.

WELL ABANDONMENT

Test holes must be abandoned when they are no longer of use; occasionally, a production well must be abandoned. This must be done properly in order to

- eliminate a physical hazard,
- prevent groundwater contamination,
- conserve the aquifer, and
- prevent mixing of desirable and undesirable water between aquifers.

The basic concept governing the proper sealing of abandoned wells is the restoration of the geologic and hydrologic conditions that existed before the well was constructed. Each well that is abandoned should be considered unique. The methods used should be those that will give the best results. Recovery of pumps, casings, screens, and other hardware is best performed by the firm that installed the well. The well construction company is also likely to be the best firm to complete the abandonment procedures properly.

SPRINGS AND INFILTRATION GALLERIES

Springs and infiltration galleries are both conduits between groundwater and surface water. They are not typically used as the water source for a public water supply because their reliability is difficult to predict and they require more effort to protect from contamination.

Springs

Springs are locations where groundwater exits the ground surface (the groundwater surface and ground surface intersect) and are generally found at the base of a hill. They can also be the result of an artesian condition in which water from a confined aquifer is under enough pressure to flow to the surface through fractures in the rock or soil. Springs generally take the form of free-flowing water from fractures in an exposed bedrock surface or embankment or as seeps in soil embankments.

Springs are difficult to protect from contamination because they are generally closely connected to surface water infiltration and because the water intake is at the ground surface. This is in contrast to deep wells, which are not typically closely connected or influenced by surface water and have pumps with intakes at depths below where animals or humans can easily access. Therefore, the spring's intake should be enclosed in a tamper-proof, vermin-proof concrete box, and the site should have diversion channels that route surface drainage around the collection site. The protective structure should be designed to prevent clogging by sediment, debris, or ice, with drains to prevent stagnation during times of low flow and with access ways to allow for periodic inspection and cleanout. Some control of chemical materials within a safe distance of the spring or within the recharge area should be maintained. Also, regulatory requirements for treatment and periodic chemical analysis are generally more stringent and costly than for well sources.

Flow rates from springs are often strongly influenced by the time of year and amount of recent precipitation. Therefore, a spring's flow should be monitored closely and be known to be reliable through the four seasons of a year and during drought years if it is to be used.

Infiltration Galleries

The purpose of an infiltration gallery is usually to collect water from a surface water source but at a point where the flow has infiltrated through a filter material, such as several feet of sand or gravel. In this way, most of the particulate matter is removed. Infiltration galleries are generally more costly to install than surface water intakes and are used in situations where the cost for primary treatment and infiltration of the surface water justifies the additional effort.

FIGURE 2–21 Example of an infiltration gallery

As illustrated in Figure 2–21, a typical infiltration gallery installation involves the construction of a trench that is parallel to a streambed and is about 10 ft (3 m) beyond the high-water mark. Perforated or open joint pipe is placed in the trench in a bed of gravel and then covered with a layer of coarse sand. The pipe and gravel can be wrapped with a geotextile filter fabric for additional filtration and to prevent silt clogging of the gravel pack. The upper part of the trench is filled with fairly impermeable material to reduce entry of surface water. The collection pipes terminate in a concrete basin from which water is pumped. Although the water collected in an infiltration gallery may be of much better quality than the surface source, it will not necessarily be free of all turbidity or pathogenic organisms. The water is therefore generally treated in compliance with state and federal requirements for surface water.

SELECTED SUPPLEMENTARY READINGS

AWWA Standard for Disinfection of Wells, ANSI/AWWA C654. Denver, Colo.: American Water Works Association (latest edition).

AWWA Standard for Water Wells, ANSI/AWWA A100. Denver, Colo.: American Water Works Association (latest edition).

Basics of Well Construction Operator's Guide. 1986. Denver, Colo.: American Water Works Association.

Borch, M.A., S.A. Smith, and L.N. Noble. 1993. *Evaluation and Restoration of Water Supply Wells*. Denver, Colo.: Awwa Research Foundation and American Water Works Association.

Driscoll, F.G. 1986. *Groundwater and Wells*. St. Paul, Minn.: Johnson Filtration Systems, Inc.

Estimated Use of Water in the United States in 1995. 1998. USGS Circular 1200. Denver, Colo.: US Geological Survey.

Manual M21, Groundwater. 1989. Denver, Colo.: American Water Works Association.

Manual of Individual Water Supply Systems. 1982. US Environmental Protection Agency, Office of Drinking Water. EPA-570/9-82-004. Washington, D.C.: US Government Printing Office.

Manual of Instruction for Water Treatment Plant Operators. 1989. Albany, N.Y.: New York State Department of Health.

Manual of Water Utility Operations, 8th ed. 1988. Austin, Tex.: Texas Water Utilities Association. Available: http://www.twua.org/publications.htm#wuo.

US Geological Survey Ground-Water Resources Program. 2001. USGS Fact Sheet 056-01. Available: http://water.usgs.gov/ogw/.

Water Quality and Treatment, 5th ed. 1999. New York: McGraw-Hill and American Water Works Association (available from AWWA).

Surface Water Sources

Surface water is the term used to describe water on the land surface. It may be running, such as in streams and rivers, or quiescent, such as in lakes, reservoirs, and ponds. Surface water is produced by runoff of precipitation and natural groundwater seepage. For regulatory purposes, surface water is defined as all water open to the atmosphere and subject to surface runoff.

Although groundwater is used as a water supply source in rural areas and by most small communities, it is rare for sufficient groundwater to be available to serve large cities. Consequently, most large population centers must be served from surface water sources. Many large cities have thrived because of the availability of fresh water. Examples include the large cities around the Great Lakes and along major rivers. When a city continues to grow in spite of insufficient groundwater or surface water available to supply public and industrial needs, it is necessary to reroute surface water to the city from other areas through canals or pipelines.

Most large population centers must be served from surface water sources.

SURFACE RUNOFF

Most surface water originates directly from precipitation in the form of rainfall or snow. Rainfall, following the path of least resistance, runs rather quickly off the land surface toward streams. The land area that drains to a certain point in a stream or river is known as its watershed or drainage area.

A watershed is surrounded by a ridge of high ground called its divide, which separates it from other watersheds.

Snow, on the other hand, contributes slowly to the surface water system and is an extremely important form of water storage. Most areas of the western United States and Canada depend on water melting from the snowpack in the mountains for a continuing supply of water during the warm months.

Groundwater from springs and seeps also contributes flow to most streams. This is often referred to as base flow. If the water table is at a level lower than the water surface of the stream, the stream will recharge the groundwater. If the adjacent water table is at a level higher than the water surface of the stream, water from the water table will flow to the stream (Figure). The pattern of flowing to or from the stream can vary according to seasonal fluctuation of the water table. Many streams would dry up shortly after a rain if it were not for groundwater flow.

Influences on Runoff

The principal factors that affect how rapidly surface water runs off the land are

- rainfall intensity,
- rainfall duration,
- soil composition,
- soil moisture,
- ground slope,
- vegetation cover, and
- human influences.

Rainfall intensity

Slow, gentle rainfall generally produces very little runoff. There is plenty of time for the rain to soak into (infiltrate) the soil. However, as rainfall intensity increases, the surface of the soil becomes saturated. Because a saturated soil can hold no more water, further rainfall builds up on the surface and begins to flow, creating surface runoff.

Rainfall duration

The duration of a rainstorm also influences the amount of runoff. Even a slow, gentle rain, if it lasts long enough, can eventually saturate the soil and allow runoff to take place.

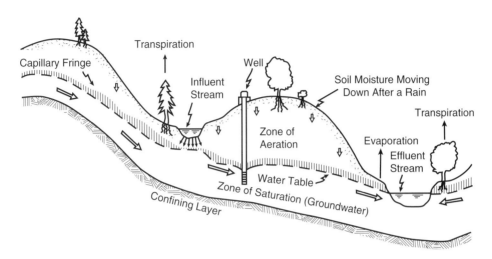

Adopted from Linsley et al. 1999.

FIGURE 3–1 Groundwater and stream interaction

Soil composition

The composition of the surface soil also has a marked effect on the amount of run-off produced. Coarse sand, for example, has large void spaces that allow water to pass through readily, so even a high-intensity rainfall on sand may result in little runoff. On the other hand, light rainfall on soil such as clay will generally result in a relatively large amount of runoff. Clay soils not only have small void spaces but they swell when wet. This expansion closes the void spaces, which further reduces the infiltration rate and results in greater surface runoff.

Soil moisture

If soil is already wet from a previous rain, surface runoff will occur sooner than if the soil were dry. Consequently, the amount of existing soil moisture has an effect on surface runoff. If the ground is frozen, it is essentially impervious, and runoff from rain or melting snow may then be up to 100 percent.

Ground slope

Ground slope has a great effect on the rate of surface runoff. Flow of water off flat land is often so slow that there is usually ample opportunity for a large portion of it to soak into the ground. But when rain falls on steeply sloping ground, as much as 80 percent of it may become surface runoff.

Vegetation cover

Vegetation covering the ground plays an important role in limiting runoff. Roots of plants and deposits of decaying natural organic litter (such as leaves, branches, or pine needles) create a porous layer above the soil and allow water to move easily into the soil. Hard, driving rains will sometimes compact bare soil, closing the void spaces. However, vegetation and organic litter act as a cover to protect soil from this compaction; they maintain the soil's water-holding and in-filtration capacity. This cover also reduces evaporation of soil moisture, though this effect is less significant.

Human influences

Human activities have a decided effect on surface water runoff. Although dams are generally built to retard the flow of runoff, most other activities and structures tend to increase the rate of flow. Canals and ditches are usually constructed to hasten flow, and agricultural activities generally remove vegetation that would naturally retard the runoff rate.

The impervious surfaces of buildings, streets, and other paved areas greatly increase the amount of runoff. By hastening the flow of surface water, flooding often occurs and the opportunity for water to percolate into the soil to replenish groundwater supplies is reduced. Many states have passed stormwater management laws requiring that infiltration practices be used to lessen the effects of increased runoff from urbanization.

Watercourses

Surface water runoff naturally flows along the path of least resistance. All of the water within a watershed flows toward one primary watercourse, unless it is diverted by a constructed watercourse such as a canal or pipeline.

Natural watercourses

Typical natural watercourses include brooks, creeks, streams, and rivers. Watercourses may flow continuously, occasionally, or intermittently, depending on the frequency of rainfall and other sources of water.

Perennial streams.   Watercourses that flow continuously at all times of the year are called perennial streams. They are generally supplied by a combination of surface runoff, springs, groundwater seepage, and possibly snowmelt.

Ephemeral streams.   Streams flowing only occasionally are called ephemeral streams (Figure 3–2). The word ephemeral refers to something that has only a

FIGURE 3–2 Bed of an ephemeral stream

brief existence. These streams usually flow only during and shortly after a rain and are supplied only by surface runoff.

Intermittent streams. Many streams fall between the other two categories. Depending on the rainfall, snowmelt, and groundwater levels, they may have running water for weeks or months at a time. These streams, which flow when groundwater levels are high, are dry at times and are known as intermittent streams.

Constructed watercourses
Many facilities are constructed to hasten the flow of surface water or to divert it in a direction other than the one in which it would flow under natural conditions. Ditches, channels, canals, aqueducts, conduits, tunnels, and pipelines are all examples. In many cases, water is diverted from its natural watershed into another.

Many local waterways are constructed to prevent water from ponding in areas where it would impede agricultural or urban development. Other examples of constructed watercourses include canals provided for boat access or shipping, aqueducts to provide irrigation water to arid regions, and pipelines to convey potable water to areas that have an insufficient natural supply.

Water Bodies

A water body is a water storage basin. It can be a natural basin, such as a pond or lake, or a reservoir constructed to serve some specific water need. Reservoirs range from small basins constructed by farmers for watering livestock to massive reservoirs that store water for public water system and recreational uses.

SURFACE SOURCE CONSIDERATIONS

The development of a surface water source for use by a public water supply requires careful study of the quantity and quality of water available.

Quantity of Water Available

The prime consideration in selecting a water source is that the supply must reliably furnish the quantity of water required. The flow in any watercourse fluctuates in relation to the amount of rainfall and runoff that occurs, so it must be known that sufficient water will be available during low-flow or drought conditions.

Community water needs are normally greatest during the warm months of summer and early fall, and this is usually the period when natural stream flow is the lowest. To compensate for this problem and increase water supply reliability, impounding reservoirs can be constructed to store water during periods of excess supply. This water can then be used during periods when natural stream flow is deficient.

Safe yield is a concept that describes the availability of water through a critical dry period. It is calculated based on the size of the impoundment, the area of the watershed, and the desired level of reliability. In simple terms, the safe yield of a watershed area represents the maximum rate at which water can be withdrawn continuously over a long period of time, including very dry periods. For example, without storage, the safe yield of a stream is simply the amount of water that can be withdrawn during a period of lowest flow. In many states, the safe yield of a direct stream withdrawal for public water supply is the "1Q30," or the lowest one-day flow that occurs on average once every 30 years.

Safe yield can be increased by the addition of storage. If a stream has a high enough flow in the winter or other season to replenish water in an impoundment, the amount of water that can be withdrawn during dry seasons can be greatly increased. There are many interrelated factors that must be considered when calculating the safe yield of a public water supply. In addition to rainfall and stream flow considerations, allowances must also be made for other uses of the source water for agricultural irrigation or by other water systems. With today's awareness for sustaining natural resources, there must also be an allowance for a portion of stream flow to pass through a reservoir to sustain downstream habitat for fish and other aquatic organisms.

Water Quality

Although it is technically possible to treat just about any poor-quality water to an acceptable quality for public water system use, it is often not economically practical. For example, it may be more cost effective to pipe water a considerable distance from a remote, good-quality supply than to treat poor-quality water that is available locally.

The economic concerns are often complex and are greatly influenced by supply and demand. There may also be political and legal considerations, such as who has the "rights" to the water. One good example is salt water, which is available to many large cities located adjacent to oceans. At this time, it is less expensive to transport fresh water from sources hundreds of miles away than to desalt ocean water. However, in areas of the world where fresh water is not sufficiently available to supply demand, desalinization is used.

The economics are changing as treatment technology improves. It is likely that the improvements in membrane technology will substantially reduce the cost of treating water from poor-quality sources in coming years.

Some of the principal quality factors that must be considered in evaluating the suitability of a water source for use are

- excessive turbidity;
- susceptibility to microbiological contamination;
- susceptibility to chemical or radiological contamination;
- taste, odor, and color;
- occurrence of algae growth; and
- water temperature.

The influences that these factors have on water use and treatability are covered in *Water Treatment* and *Water Quality*, other titles in this series.

WATER STORAGE

Water can be stored by natural means, in impoundments, or by recharging natural aquifers.

Natural Storage

Natural lakes are often used as a source for public water supply. Natural lakes occur most often in glaciated regions. Large lakes such as the Great Lakes of North America were formed by the movement of massive lobes of ice that left deep, wide valleys after the glaciers receded. The melting of large ice blocks that had been earlier stranded by the receding glaciers formed smaller lakes (called kettles).

Generally, a lake must be relatively isolated from human activities to have good water quality. Lakes having a watershed with heavy agricultural activity, industrial operations, or urban areas are often highly polluted.

If a lake located some distance from a community is being considered for use, it must be decided whether it is better to treat the water at the source and then pipe the finished water to the community or to pipe the raw water to the community and treat it there. Because of the considerable cost of piping water over long distances, an engineering analysis of all the alternatives must be made.

Impoundments

An impoundment is a human-made lake created either by excavating a basin in soil or by building a dam across a stream valley. Although there is evidence of dam construction as far back as 4000 BC (Nile River), dams were not widely used until the mid-1800s. Dams were first used primarily for water supply and to harness river flow for mills. In glaciated regions, dams and perimeter berms have been used to increase the depth and storage capacity of kettle lakes. With the development of modern construction equipment and techniques, dams have become a common way of creating a large reservoir. They are usually built where damming a valley stream or river can form the reservoir. The deeper and narrower the valley, the more economical it is to construct the dam. Dams are generally constructed of earth, rock, or concrete.

Offstream reservoirs can be constructed next to major rivers to add storage to a water system. Water can be pumped from the river to the reservoir during high-flow periods, then withdrawn for water supply during low-flow periods. This type of impoundment is commonly referred to as a pumped-storage reservoir and can involve constructing a dam across the stream of a small tributary, thereby avoiding many of the adverse environmental impacts of building a dam on a major river.

Types of dams

Dams are classified according to the type of material they are constructed from and how they resist the pressure forces imposed on them. The four general types of dams are gravity, arch, buttress, and embankment (Figure 3–3). The first three types are typically constructed of concrete; embankment dams are constructed either of earthfill or rockfill. A gravity dam depends on its self-weight to resist both sliding and overturning. In a buttress dam, which is a type of gravity dam, buttresses support reinforced concrete slabs and the impounded water's weight is used to help resist sliding and overturning. In contrast, an arch dam resists movement by transferring the thrust of water pressure to the rock walls of a canyon.

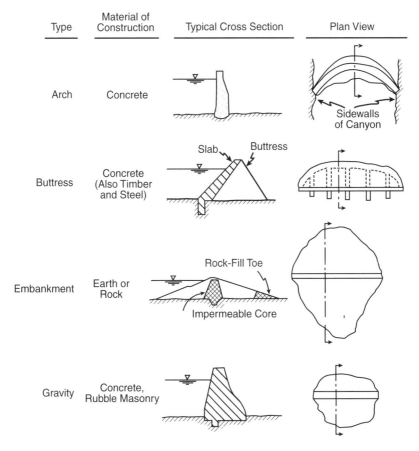

Adapted from Linsley et al. 1999.

FIGURE 3–3 Types of dams

Dams constructed of earth and rock, called embankment dams, are the most common type of dam. They must be carefully engineered to resist the forces of the reservoir water and prevent damage or failure due to seepage or undermining.

A cross section of a typical earth dam and intake tower is shown in Figure 3–4. An embankment dam may be constructed mostly of sandy or rocky soils if locally available, but there must be an inner core of impermeable material to ensure water tightness. Earth dams often require an internal drainage system (using sand and gravel) to reduce water pressure in the dam, which in turn helps prevent "internal erosion" of soils from within the earth dam.

Rockfill dams are another type of embankment dam. Rockfill dams use a broad range of rock sizes to provide stability, with water tightness provided by building a reinforced concrete slab on the upstream face of the dam.

Dam design

The subsurface conditions are among the most important considerations in dam construction. The soil below the dam must have sufficient strength and be impermeable enough that the dam will not fail because of undermining. Subsurface conditions are investigated using core borings. If necessary, unsafe material must be removed and replaced with suitable material before the dam is constructed.

The design of a dam should incorporate use of locally available materials. An earth dam is typically used where there is an abundance of soil material and where bedrock is very deep. A concrete dam is often used where soil is scarce and/or bedrock is shallow.

Some small reservoirs have sufficient capacity to hold all water that flows into them, so no outlet is necessary. However, because most dams are constructed across a stream or river, they are expected to overflow at least occasionally, especially during flood conditions. The design of the dam outlet, or spillway, is particularly

FIGURE 3–4 Cross section of dam and intake tower for impounded surface water supply

important in regulating the flow from a reservoir. The spillway must allow safe release of unusually heavy flows from the reservoir. If water should overflow the top of an embankment dam, it could cause a washout that will severely damage or destroy the dam.

Simply put, a spillway is a portion of the dam built at a lower level, which will overflow during a flood. Most spillways are free-overflow structures, since water freely flows over its crest as the pool rises during a flood. The spillway "crest" typically defines the "normal pool" of the reservoir. Figure 3–5 shows a concrete chute spillway on the abutment of an earth dam. Other spillways consist of gates that must be raised to allow water to flow through the dam (Figure 3–6).

To ensure a reliable water system, dams for water supply should be designed to pass at least a 100-year flood event, which has a 1 percent chance of occurrence in any given year. However, if failure of the dam could cause loss of life to people downstream, it should be designed for a larger flood. In many states, such dams must be designed to pass the "probable maximum flood," which can be up to five times the size of a 100-year flood. Nearly all states have dam safety regulations that stipulate the standards that dams must meet.

Dam maintenance

Most very large dams have been constructed with federal funds and remain under federal ownership. Others are owned by the state or local jurisdiction or solely by a water utility.

In cases where a dam is owned by a water utility, the system operator may have responsibility for dam maintenance. The structure must periodically be inspected and maintained to prevent failure. Failure of a dam can result in both

FIGURE 3–5 Yellow Creek Dam. Intake structure is to the left of the dam, and chute spillway is to the right of the dam

FIGURE 3-6 Chute spillway on a concrete dam

loss of a water source and destruction of downstream property. Water-control structures such as spillways and slide gates require periodic maintenance to keep them in good working order and to prevent failure.

Careful records should be kept of all inspections and work done on dams and water-control structures. Most states have specific procedures and reports that must be followed and maintained on dam maintenance. These and other normal inspection and maintenance procedures should be documented in an operation and maintenance manual.

Decreasing numbers of dams have been built in recent years, primarily because of public concern with regard to the environmental damage caused by flooding areas of scenic beauty and disrupting wildlife habitats.

Groundwater Recharge

Some attempts have been made to provide water storage by recharging depleted groundwater aquifers. Methods to accomplish this include providing large basins to allow the water to infiltrate the soil and the direct injection of water.

If untreated surface water is to be injected into the soil, care must be taken not to pollute the aquifer. In addition, turbidity in the injected water will gradually plug the injection area. Therefore, injection water must generally be fully treated to drinking water quality before it can be injected. Another problem with using recharge as a means of storing water is that the volume of water pumped into the aquifer cannot always be fully recovered.

In recent years, there has been increasing objection to the construction of new surface reservoirs for a variety of environmental reasons. In some cases, projects have been approved by local regulatory agencies, but the plans have been vetoed by the US Environmental Protection Agency. When storage of large quantities of water is necessary but the creation of new surface impoundments is completely unacceptable, the options will be either to pipe water for long distances to where a reservoir is acceptable or to store water in underground aquifers. As a result, aquifer recharge may become more common in the future.

All injection of fluids into the ground is now subject to state approval under the rules of the federal Underground Injection Control Program.

INTAKE STRUCTURES

Water is removed from a surface impoundment or stream by an intake structure. Types of intake structures include simple surface inlets, submerged intakes, movable intakes, pump intakes, and infiltration galleries.

Surface Intakes

In the simplest form, a surface intake consists of a small concrete structure, which contains a slide gate or stop log, and is situated at the bank of a river or lake. When the slide gate or stop log is removed, water spills into a canal, ditch, or pipeline, which then carries the water to the treatment plant. Larger installations may consist of a structure that has a bar screen and methods of removing accumulated trash from the screen.

The principal disadvantage of using a surface intake on a river or reservoir is that water quality is not usually as good as it would be below the surface. The water may be warmer in summer; have ice on the surface in winter; and may have algae, leaves, logs, and other floating debris at the surface at certain times of the year. If the elevation of the water in the lake or stream fluctuates, there is also the problem of locating a surface intake so that it will draw water under all conditions.

Many surface water treatment plants that normally draw water from a submerged intake also have an emergency surface, or "shore," intake. In the event of plugging or other failure of their submerged intake, the surface intake can be activated to furnish water of usable quality while repairs are made.

Submerged Intakes

Submerged intakes draw water from below the surface. The best water quality in most lakes and streams can usually be obtained in deep water. Intakes should not be located directly on the bottom or they will draw in silt and sand; therefore, they are often raised a short distance above the bottom. Submerged intakes have the advantages of presenting no surface obstruction to navigation and being less likely to be damaged by floating debris and ice. There are many designs used for submerged intakes; one typical type is illustrated in Figure 3–7. In some instances, screens with very fine openings are used to prevent fish from being drawn into the intake (Figure 3–8).

FIGURE 3-7 Schematic of a typical submerged intake

FIGURE 3-8 Fish screen for a submerged intake

Movable Intakes

Water from shallow depths may be quite warm in summer and may also have heavy algae growths. At these times, water drawn from deeper levels is more likely to be free of these problems.

On the other hand, deep water in lakes and reservoirs can sometimes develop poor quality in winter as a result of stratification, which occurs when colder, denser water sinks to the bottom. Then, oxygen depletion and the dissolving of nuisance chemicals from bottom sediment can produce serious taste-and-odor problems. However, water drawn from higher levels is more likely to be free of these problems.

Movable intakes are used in lakes and streams where the water levels vary greatly or where there are other reasons for varying the depth of withdrawing water. Movable intakes are also used where good foundation is lacking or where other conditions prevent the construction of a more substantial structure.

Intake structures that have multiple inlet ports are also used in locations where the water level or water quality varies (Figure 3–9). By opening and closing valves, the operator can withdraw or mix water from several different depths to compensate for changing water elevation, to avoid ice cover, or to select the depth from which the best-quality water can be withdrawn.

FIGURE 3–9 Intake structure with multiple inlet ports

Pump Intakes

Pump intakes are used where it is not possible to construct a facility that will allow water to flow from the source by gravity. One design, illustrated in Figure 3–10, has an intake pump and suction piping mounted on a dolly that runs on tracks. As the water level rises or falls, sections of discharge piping are removed or added and the rail car is moved accordingly.

Infiltration Galleries

An infiltration gallery is an intake that collects seepage water. It is usually located next to a lake or river where it can pick up seepage from the surrounding sand. A "buried intake" (instead of an open intake) can similarly be located in the bottom of a lake or stream but it can be used only if the bottom sand is porous enough and has the proper gradation to provide a reasonable flow rate. There must also be enough wave action or flow across the bottom to prevent the accumulation of silt, which would plug the sand surface.

Where the proper conditions are present for installing an infiltration system, infiltration galleries will usually provide water of much better quality than water taken directly from the source because the natural straining action of the sand eliminates debris and reduces turbidity levels. They also have the advantages of not freezing or icing and they are not as vulnerable to damage.

SURFACE SUPPLY OPERATING PROBLEMS

Surface water sources can have a number of physical, chemical, and biological problems that are troublesome for the water system operator.

FIGURE 3-10 Movable pump intake

Stream Contamination

Streams in particular are at the mercy of all upstream users of the water and land within the drainage basin. Rivers of commerce such as the Ohio and Mississippi are often in the news because of spills from barges, leaks from tank facilities, broken pipelines, accidental industrial spills, and other assaults on stream water quality. Utilities using particularly vulnerable streams as a water source generally depend on warning systems to give advance notice of problems approaching their intake. Some streams also have occasional periods when water quality is especially poor as a result of natural causes, such as heavy spring runoff.

Any water system that is vulnerable to poor-quality episodes should construct adequate storage facilities. These facilities are then used when the intake is shut down due to poor-quality water passing the intake point.

Lake Contamination

Lakes and reservoirs are also vulnerable to natural and human contamination. One problem encountered by some water systems using reservoirs in agricultural areas is the occasional occurrence of nitrate levels exceeding state and federal standards. The nitrates are caused by runoff from farmlands located in the drainage basin; they may persist for several months each year. High sediment loads carrying phosphorus, a common nutrient, are also a problem in agricultural basins and those undergoing urbanization.

Excessive growth of algae and aquatic weeds in reservoirs is also quite common, particularly in warmer climates. High levels of nutrients in the water usually cause this, but the problem can be minimized by proper treatment.

A recent threat introduced to the Great Lakes by commercial shipping is the zebra mussel. This organism grows profusely in intake structures and can quickly reduce water flow if not controlled. Another mussel, the quagga, has been found to cause similar problems. These organisms are gradually being transported to other surface water impoundments by boats and birds. It appears that they will probably become established as permanent nuisance organisms in most waters of North America.

Control of aquatic plants, prevention of lake stratification, control of mussels, and other treatment of source water are detailed in *Water Treatment*, also part of this series.

Icing

Operators in cold-weather areas often face the additional operational problems of frazil ice or anchor ice. When the water is almost at the freezing point and is rapidly being cooled, small, disk-shaped frazil ice crystals will form and be distributed throughout the water mass. When the frazil crystals are carried to the depth of a water intake, they may adhere to the intake screen and quickly build up to a solid plug across the opening.

Anchor ice is slightly different in that it is composed of sheetlike crystals that adhere to and grow on submerged objects. Although experience varies at different locations, most systems experience ice blocking only at night. The conditions that have generally been found to be favorable to ice crystal formation are

- clear skies at night (because there will be high heat loss by radiation),
- air temperature of less than 19.4°F (–7°C),
- daytime water temperature not greater than 32.4°F (0.2°C), and
- winds greater than 10 mph (16 kph) at the water surface.

A falling level in the intake will usually indicate icing of an intake well. It is generally best to stop using the intake immediately when icing is noticed because the blockage will only get worse. If sufficient storage is available or another intake can be used, the easiest method of ridding the intake of ice is to just wait and let it float off within a few hours.

Water systems that frequently experience icing have tried such things as providing the intake with piping to backflush the line with settled water or blowing the line with compressed air or steam. If more than one intake is available, alternating intakes will allow any accumulated ice to melt and float away from the intake opening.

Methods of constructing new intake structures to minimize ice formation include using very widely spaced screening or no screen at all and using nonferrous materials such as fiberglass for the intake pipe and structures. Many intakes are also designed to keep the entrance velocity very low by using large bell-shaped structures or several inlets.

Stream source intakes are not ordinarily deep enough to allow water to be taken from a depth beneath the supercooled level, so multiple intake points and use of heat may be necessary to prevent icing.

Evaporation and Seepage

Surface water reservoirs lose water to evaporation and seepage. Evaporation loss can range from less than 2 ft (0.6 m) per year in the northern part of the United States to more than 6 ft (2 m) in the southwestern United States. Seepage losses occur through the bottom and sides of the impoundment and can vary greatly depending on soil type, geology, and location of the lake surface relative to the surrounding groundwater table. These losses cannot economically be controlled in large reservoirs, so the reservoirs are generally designed larger than required to compensate for the expected loss.

In small, excavated reservoirs, seepage can be controlled by lining the impoundment with compacted clay or a synthetic liner. Evaporation can also be controlled by covering a reservoir with floating plastic sheets (Figure 3–11) or applying a thin layer of a liquid chemical to the surface.

Siltation

All streams carry sediment. Most of this sediment is deposited when water loses velocity upstream from a dam. The rate of siltation is generally a function of both the type of soil in the area and how well the land is protected by vegetation. In some locations, siltation is so rapid that most of the capacity of a dam reservoir is lost within a few years after it is constructed.

The problem of siltation can never be completely solved, but through better land-use management it can be minimized. Enforcement of rules governing good

Courtesy of Burke Environmental Products, a Division of Burke Industries, Inc.

FIGURE 3–11 Reservoir cover installed on Garvey Reservoir at Monterey Park Metropolitan Water District of Los Angeles, Calif.

practice in farming, logging, road construction, and other operations that disturb the land will help reduce the amount of sediment entering tributary streams.

Creation of artificial wetlands for small streams or at the upper ends of a reservoir can also help reduce siltation. The reduction in the stream's velocity caused by the wetlands allows the bulk of the sediment load to drop out in the wetlands before the water reaches the impoundment. Water quality is improved since many nutrients that adhere to sediment are also removed by the wetlands.

When the capacity of a reservoir has been decreased by siltation, there are three general options: the silt can be removed by dredging, the reservoir can be drained and the silt excavated, or a new reservoir can be constructed. Draining and excavating are only an option when the water system has other water sources available, and constructing a new reservoir is only possible if the necessary additional land is available. A cost analysis of the available options must be made to decide how best to restore the lost reservoir capacity.

SELECTED SUPPLEMENTARY READINGS

Linsley, R.K. et al. 1992. *Water Resources Engineering.* New York: McGraw-Hill, Inc.

Manual of Individual Water Supply Systems. 1982. US Environmental Protection Agency, Office of Drinking Water. EPA-570/9-82-004. Washington, D.C.: US Government Printing Office.

Manual of Instruction for Water Treatment Plant Operators. 1989. Albany, N.Y.: New York State Department of Health.

Manual of Water Utility Operations, 8th ed. 1988. Austin, Tex.: Texas Water Utilities Association. Available: http://www.twua.org/publications.htm#wuo.

Water Quality and Treatment, 5th ed. 1999. New York: McGraw-Hill and American Water Works Association (available from AWWA).

4

Emergency and Alternative Water Sources

An emergency response plan should be developed by each utility.

It is important that service to a public water system be continuous and uninterrupted. The most important reason for maintaining continuity of service is for protection of public health. Any loss of system pressure or interruption in service is an opportunity for microbiological or chemical contamination to enter the water system. In addition, lack of water for sanitary purposes for more than a short period of time can create problems with disease. The possibility of water contamination or loss of the normal water source requires that every water utility develop an emergency response plan.

Table 4–1 illustrates a disaster effects matrix for a typical utility. It lists the disasters that can affect a water system and the potential magnitude of the hazards associated with those disasters. More information on emergency planning is contained in AWWA Manual M19, *Emergency Planning for Water Utilities*.

An emergency response plan should be developed by each utility in cooperation with neighboring utilities and with the appropriate local and state agencies. These other agencies include local police, fire, and emergency or disaster preparedness departments, as well as the same groups at the county and state levels. The purpose of this chapter is not to address the entire emergency planning program but only to study possible emergencies involving source water. Alternative water sources for nonpotable use are also discussed.

TABLE 4–1 Hazard summary for a hypothetical water system

Type of Hazard	Estimated Probability	Estimated Magnitude	Comments
Earthquake	1 in 60 years	7.0 (Richter scale)	
Fault rupture	Medium	2 ft (0.6 m)	Meridian fault
Ground shaking	High		
Liquefaction	Medium–low	Vertical and horizontal accelerations	Fill areas
Densification	Medium		Fill areas
Landslide	Medium–high		In slopes of 30 percent
Tsunami and seiche	None		
Hurricane	None		
Wind			
Storm surge			
Flooding			
Tornado	Low		
Flood	Low–medium	100-year flood to elevation = 1,020 ft (311 m)	At treatment plant
Forest or brush fire	High		Dry Creek watershed
Volcanic eruption	1 in 300 years	150 miles away (241 km)	Mount Nueces
Other severe weather			
Snow or ice	None		
Extreme heat	High	100-year drought	Reservoirs depleted
Wind	Medium	60–80 mph (97–129 km/hr)	Usually in winter
Lightning	Low		
Other			
Waterborne disease	Low		Cryptosporidiosis

Table continued next page

TABLE 4–1 Hazard summary for a hypothetical water system *(continued)*

Type of Hazard	Estimated Probability	Estimated Magnitude	Comments
Hazardous-material release			
Chlorine	Medium–high	1-ton containers	Earthquake damage
Other spill	Medium	Tanker car	Dry Creek reservoir
Structural fire	Low		
Construction accident	Medium	Line damage	In older area of system
Road	Low		
Rail	Medium		Rail yard near warehouse
Water	Low		
Air	Low		
Nuclear power plant accident	Low	Contamination	Lake West reservoir
Nuclear bomb explosion	Low		
Vandalism, terrorism	Medium		Storage tanks
Riot	Low		
Strike	Low		

CAUSES OF SOURCE DISRUPTION

In general, catastrophes that can disrupt the operation of a water source fall into the following two categories: natural disasters, including earthquakes (Figures 4–1 and 4–2), floods, hurricanes, tornadoes, forest fires, landslides, snow and ice storms, and tidal waves; and human activities, including vandalism, explosions, strikes, riots, terrorism, warfare, and water contamination caused by leaks, spills, or dumping of hazardous materials. In addition, there is always the possibility of major equipment failure and breakdown caused by human error.

For whatever reason the water source is disrupted, the water can effectively become unusable because it could be so contaminated that it is far beyond the ability of available equipment to treat it to acceptable quality. In addition, the water may no longer be available from the source as a result of complete mechanical failure of the treatment and distribution systems.

Source: M.J. O'Rourke, RPI, NCEER.

FIGURE 4–1 A 400,000-gal (1.5-million-L) steel tank uplifted during the 1992 Landers, Calif., earthquake

Sources of Contamination

Microbiological, chemical, or radiological agents can contaminate source water. Both groundwater and surface water sources are vulnerable. Some relatively common examples of contamination incidents are

- a pipeline that has broken upstream of a surface water intake, allowing several hundred gallons (liters) of fuel oil to be spilled into the river;
- a tank truck that has overturned on a bridge and has spilled a quantity of toxic chemical into the river; and
- a spill of chemical solvent on the ground near a well that has penetrated to the aquifer and is now showing up in the well at increasing concentrations.

When contamination of a water source occurs, the first thing that must be determined is the length of time for the contamination episode. In the above examples, the tank truck spill will probably pass the river intake in a matter of hours. The fuel oil spill could last for several days. The aquifer contamination, on the other hand, could be permanent; if it will pass by naturally or can be cleaned up, the process may still take years. When source water becomes contaminated, a utility can

Source: D.B. Ballantyne.

FIGURE 4–2 Flocculator/clarifier center mechanism damaged during 1989 Loma Prieta earthquake

stop drawing water and operate on stored water until the episode is over, change to an alternative water supply until the episode is over, or treat the contaminated water.

Most chemical contaminants in water can be reduced to acceptable levels with the proper type of treatment, such as aeration or carbon adsorption. Microbiological contaminants can generally be controlled by proper coagulation, sedimentation, and filtration treatment plus heavy doses of disinfectant. However, the equipment required for this special treatment may not be required for normal source treatment. Water system operators should therefore consider the contamination problems that might occur and have the special equipment available or make plans to obtain it quickly if needed. Additional details on water treatment methods for contaminant removal are included in *Water Treatment*, also part of this series.

Notification of Possible Contamination

Utilities should work with their local emergency planning department prior to any incident to coordinate specific procedures for contacting local, state, and federal officials when an incident occurs. If the contamination is a result of an intentional act, utilities should also notify local law enforcement, as well as state and federal authorities. Further information is available from the US Environmental Protection Agency's *Guidance for Water Utility Response, Recovery, and Remediation Actions for Man-made and/or Technological Emergencies.*

Loss of Water Source

A complete (temporary or permanent) loss of a water source could occur when an earthquake has damaged all of a water system's wells, when a flash flood on a river has destroyed a system's intake facilities, or from system failures such as a pipeline break or tunnel collapse.

If a water system's usual water source is no longer available because of mechanical disruption, the first decision is whether the facility is repairable or if temporary facilities can be installed. For example, the damaged wells may not be repairable, in which case new wells may have to be drilled, and that could take months. If a surface water intake is destroyed, it may be possible to install a temporary pipeline or bring in portable pumps. These tasks might be accomplished in a few days.

Short-term options

The following short-term options should be considered when a water source is damaged or destroyed:

- If a limited supply of water is still available, commence conservation or rationing.
- Supply customers with water from tank trucks.
- Supply customers with bottled water.
- Draw water from adjoining water systems.

Long-term options

The following long-term options should be considered when a water source is damaged or destroyed:

- Drill new wells.
- Construct a new surface water source.
- Clean up the source of contamination.
- Install a connection to purchase water from another water system.
- Impose permanent conservation requirements.
- Develop additional sources for nonpotable uses.

- Reuse wastewater for nonpotable requirements.
- Install a dual potable–nonpotable water system.
- Construct new raw water storage, such as a new reservoir.
- Perform aquifer recharge.

Evaluating the options

There are many factors that must be considered and information that must be gathered before choosing a specific emergency option. Some of these concerns are as follows:

- Technical and logistical feasibility
  - What procedures are required to implement the option?
  - Is the required technology available and properly developed?
  - How much water can the option provide?
  - Will the option meet only the system's priority water needs?
  - Can it meet the system's current total water needs?
  - Can it be expanded to meet future community water needs?
  - How quickly can the option be made operational?
  - What equipment and supplies are needed?
- Reliability
  - How reliable is the option?
  - Does it require special operation and maintenance skills?
- Political considerations
  - What administrative procedures are required to implement the option?
  - Is property ownership a problem?
  - Will the option be acceptable to the public?
- Cost considerations
  - What is the initial investment required?
  - What will the operating costs be?
  - Who will bear the cost of the design, construction, and operation of the option?

ALTERNATIVE WATER SOURCES

Review of the many alternatives and considerations that must be made after an emergency emphasizes why advanced planning should be done to determine what options a water system has in the event of a disaster. Most systems do not have readily available alternative sources, so some thought and planning must be given to how water can be provided if the major water source is contaminated or must be out of service for a prolonged period of time. If at all possible, an alternative water source should be provided in advance, rather than after the emergency happens. Additional sources of material to assist in preparing for both natural and man-made disasters are given in the list of Selected Supplementary Readings at the end of this chapter. Some typical alternative sources that should be considered are discussed below.

- Surface water systems
  - Provide two or more intakes at different locations in the lake or stream.
  - Provide intakes in more than one water source, if possible.
  - Construct wells for backup of the surface source.
- Groundwater systems
  - Provide enough wells to meet demand when one or more wells are out of service.
  - Locate wells in different aquifers or far enough apart in the same aquifer so that contamination affecting one well will not affect other wells.
  - Provide a surface water emergency source.
- All systems
  - Establish interconnection with other water systems, with sufficient capacity to meet at least minimum needs.

Many potential emergencies can be averted or minimized by making preparations in advance. For instance, good security at water facilities can reduce vandalism; providing standby power eliminates complete dependence on commercial electric power; and locating all facilities far enough away from floodplains can prevent many contamination problems. In addition to averting problems that can possibly be prevented, water system operators should be prepared to act swiftly and efficiently in the event of an emergency.

INTERSYSTEM CONNECTION

In urban and suburban areas, it is quite common to find water utilities that have individual water sources and also have distribution systems that are located close to one another at some points. Even without prior planning, emergency connections can be made between the distribution systems using fire hoses or temporary piping. Unfortunately, this is time consuming in an emergency and will usually provide only a fraction of the water needed.

Efforts should be made in advance to interconnect adjoining distribution systems or, if practical, the raw water transmission systems themselves. If water mains are large enough at adjacent points and water pressure is about the same, the interconnection can be relatively simple.

The managers of adjoining water systems should carefully plan for either system to furnish water to the other in an emergency. Water system managers should first determine whether the separate water supply systems have a compatible water chemistry and quality to allow intermingling. A satisfactory connection will also require some piping to connect with feeder mains of sufficient size to provide the needed amount of water in either direction. It may also be necessary to install pressure-reducing valves and a booster station if system pressures are not compatible. It may also be desirable to provide meters for flow in either direction, for purposes of either reimbursement or just water accountability.

EMERGENCY PROVISION OF WATER

Tank trucks and bottled water can provide emergency sources of water. Rationing can be used if the supply is reduced but the distribution system is still operating.

Tank Trucks

If a water distribution system suffers massive failure and no alternative source is available, nonpiped water must be used. Tank trucks (Figure 4–3) can be used for this purpose, and every utility should maintain a record of where suitable units are available. The utility must be assured of the chemical and biological suitability of the trucks and must take precautions such as ensuring that adequate disinfection is maintained.

If the water utility does not supply the driver, it must have assurance that the driver uses recognized basic sanitary precautions and, most importantly, that he or she draws water from an acceptable water source. If water is to be taken from a neighboring utility, communication and monitoring are necessary to ensure that the water-filling point is satisfactory to both utilities.

Bottled Water

Bottled water is also frequently made available to customers when a water system fails or the water is contaminated. The demand will quickly exceed the normal supply, so arrangements must be made for supplemental supplies. In some cases, local dairies and beverage bottlers will provide water in milk cartons or bottles during an emergency.

In general, the public's use of bottled water for drinking and some cooking has been steadily increasing. Public perception that tap water may not be safe has been

Source: Ray Sato.

FIGURE 4–3 Emergency potable water provided by tanker truck in Kauai, Hawaii

part of the reason for the increased use of bottled water, as have taste, odor, and other quality objections. It is the responsibility of water utility operators and managers to provide water that is safe and palatable. Safety can never be compromised, and palatability should be a goal held constantly in mind, if not already achieved.

Bottled water can definitely be helpful in certain emergency or disaster situations. This does not have to imply the need to buy expensive brands or import water from great distances. Beverage companies in nearby communities not affected by the emergency can be called on to help. They will usually have a supply or ready source of containers and also the distribution facilities in the form of special trucks.

It is important to note that bottled water cannot be used as a substitute for making a public water supply meet the standards of regulatory agencies.

Water Rationing

For some disasters, a reduced supply of water results, but the distribution system is still functioning. Typical situations include the following:

- The system can reestablish the water source soon and has enough water in storage to supply basic customer needs if use is drastically reduced.

- An interconnection has been established with another utility but it provides only enough water to supply basic needs.
- The water system must operate at very low pressure because of pump failure or other problem. Care should be taken if the system operates at a low water pressure because the risk of contamination is higher due to backflow or groundwater infiltration.

In these cases, a severely reduced demand can help alleviate the crisis. The utility's conservation plan or emergency response plan should have all categories of water use rated. This situation is comparable to that faced by communities with severe or critical drought conditions. Table 4–2 is an example of a plan prepared for use in such situations.

WATER REUSE

As populations grow and potable water becomes scarcer in some areas, increasing consideration must be given to water reuse. The three ways in which water reuse is currently considered are indirect reuse, direct reuse, and provision of dual water systems.

Indirect Reuse

Indirect potable reuse—the use of water from streams that have upstream discharges of wastewater—has been in existence for a very long time. For instance, the discharges from individual septic systems infiltrate into aquifers, and at some later time the same water is withdrawn from wells. Sewage and industrial wastes discharged to rivers are diluted and somewhat treated by natural processes, and the water is later withdrawn by downstream communities for water supply use. Every day millions of people worldwide consume water that is partially reuse water.

At present there is no alternative for this situation and it is likely to increase as urban populations increase. As long as both the dischargers and receivers are aware of what is happening and treat the wastewater and the potable water to meet appropriate stream and drinking water standards, the situation is definitely better than unplanned reuse.

Recharging of groundwater by surface spreading or direct injection of reuse water is being practiced on a large scale in some areas. The groundwater can then be pumped for nonpotable uses, in which case demand on the potable water aquifer is reduced.

TABLE 4-2 Example of a drought or emergency conservation plan

Stage	Degree of Drought or Emergency	Consumption Reduction Goal,%	Public Information Action	Public-Sector Action	User Restrictions	Penalties for Noncompliance
I	Minor	10	Explain drought or emergency conditions. Disseminate technical information. Explain other stages and possible actions. Distribute retrofit kits at central depots. Request voluntary reduction.	Increase enforcement of hydrant-opening regulations. Increase meter-reading efficiency and meter maintenance. Implement intensive leak detection and repair program.	Voluntary installation of retrofit kits. Restriction of outside water use for landscape irrigation, washing cars, and other uses.	Warning
II	Moderate	15–18	Use media intensively to explain emergency. Explain restrictions and penalties. Explain actions in potential later stages. Request voluntary reduction.	Reduce water usage for main flushing, street flushing, public fountains, and park irrigation.	Mandatory restriction on all outside uses by residential users, except landscape irrigation. Prohibit unnecessary outside uses by any commercial users.	1. Warning 2. House call 3. Installation of flow restrictor 4. Shutoff and reconnection fee

Table continued next page

TABLE 4-2 Example of a drought or emergency conservation plan (continued)

Stage	Degree of Drought or Emergency	Consumption Reduction Goal, %	Public Information Action	Public-Sector Action	User Restrictions	Penalties for Noncompliance
III	Severe	25–30	Public officials appeal for water use reduction. Explain actions and consequences of emergency.	Prohibit all public water uses not required for health or safety.	Severely restrict all outside water use. Prohibit serving water in restaurants. Prohibit use of water-cooled air conditioners without recirculation.	Same as Stage II
IV	Critical	50 or more	Same as Stage III	Reduce system pressure to minimum permissible levels. Close public water-using activities not required for health or safety.	Prohibit all outside water use and selected commercial and industrial uses. Terminate service to selected portions of system as last extreme measure.	Same as Stage II

Direct Reuse

A large potential source of additional water for water-short areas of the world is the direct reuse of wastewater for purposes not requiring potable water. Wastewater may include treated municipal sewage, industrial cooling and process water, and agricultural irrigation runoff water. Any water that is used again after being used by any consumer is classified as reclaimed water. At the present time, the principal use of reclaimed water is for agricultural irrigation. Figure 4–4 shows a typical irrigation concept using reclaimed water. For decades, certain areas of the United States, such as the southwestern states, have successfully been applying reclaimed water to golf courses, orchards, and nonedible crops and using it for flushing toilets (Figure 4–5).

The use of wastewater for potable purposes is not generally considered acceptable at the present time. The American Water Works Association opposes the direct use of reclaimed wastewater as a potable water supply source until more research can be completed. Cost-effective treatment technology and monitoring techniques are not typically available to ensure that all processed wastewater is completely safe for human consumption.

Dual Water Systems

One method of achieving water reuse is to deliver potable water and nonpotable water to consumers through separate distribution systems. This is generally referred

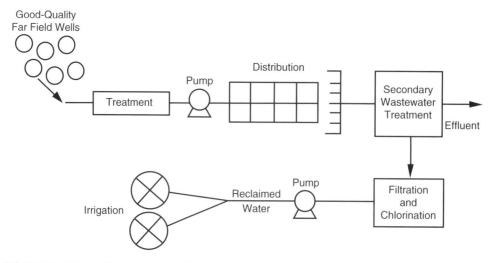

FIGURE 4–4 Irrigation concept using reclaimed water

FIGURE 4–5 El Tovar Lodge in Grand Canyon Village, Ariz., the site of the first US dual distribution system in the United States (reclaimed water is used for landscaping and toilet flushing)

to as using a dual water system. Use of a dual system is also a possible solution where potable water is in very limited supply but lower quality, nonpotable water is more plentiful. The concept is not new and has been used occasionally by water systems having unusual source water conditions.

Analyzing water demand, especially domestic use, gives a better picture of the potential for the great savings of potable water through the use of dual water systems. Within the home, high-quality potable water is needed for drinking, cooking, bathing, laundry, and dishwashing. The other uses, primarily toilet flushing, do not necessarily require high-quality water.

Exterior water use as a percentage of total use varies dramatically with the seasons. On an annual basis, exterior use averages 7 percent in Pennsylvania and 44 percent in California. Because high-quality water is not required for exterior residential uses, the demand can be satisfied by the use of nonpotable water.

There are a number of areas in the United States where dual water systems are in use; for example, Tucson and Phoenix, Ariz.; Irvine, Calif.; and Colorado Springs and Denver, Colo.

Probably the most extensive system is in St. Petersburg, Fla.; Figure 4–6 shows its water reclamation plant. The local water supply there was exhausted in 1928 because of saltwater intrusion into the water system wells. Since that time, other well fields have been developed, some as far as 50 mi (80 km) away. A great portion of the water use in the city is for irrigation of domestic lawns, as well as municipal and institutional lawns and green spaces. A very detailed financial study was undertaken comparing the cost of various alternatives. Overall savings after installing a dual water system—which include the savings from not having to develop more potable-water source capacity—are more than 6 percent. An added benefit arising from the nature of the dual system is the savings on fertilizer costs. For example, the amount of nitrogen, phosphorus, and potassium in the reuse water reduced fertilizer costs on one golf course alone by $6,000 annually.

It is likely that more dual systems will be constructed in the future, but public health consideration must be paramount. Improper use of nonpotable water must be controlled, cross-connections strictly monitored, and responsibility for the nonpotable system clearly established. NON-POTABLE MAIN REPAIRS WOULD SUCK!

Source: St. Petersburg Department of Public Utilities.

FIGURE 4–6 Reclamation plant in St. Petersburg, Fla., that incorporates secondary treatment, filtration, and chlorination

SELECTED SUPPLEMENTARY READINGS

Drinking Water System, Emergency Response Guidebook. 2001. Salt Lake City, Utah: Department of Environmental Quality, Division of Drinking Water.

Guidance for Water Utility Response, Recovery and Remediation Actions for Man-made and/or Technological Emergencies. 2002. EPA 810-R-02-001. Washington, D.C.: US Environmental Protection Agency, Office of Water, Water Protection Task Force.

Guide to Ground-Water Supply Contingency Planning for Local and State Governments. 1991. Washington, D.C.: US Environmental Protection Agency, Office of Drinking Water.

Manual M19, Emergency Planning for Water Utility Management. 2001. Denver, Colo.: American Water Works Association.

Manual M24, Dual Water Systems. 1994. Denver, Colo.: American Water Works Association.

Minimizing Earthquake Damage: A Guide for Water Utilities. 1994. Denver, Colo.: American Water Works Association.

Security Analysis and Response for Water Utilities. 2001. Denver, Colo.: American Water Works Association.

Water System Security: A Field Guide. 2002. Denver, Colo.: American Water Works Association.

Use and Conservation of Water

The utility and water system operators must make sure that every gallon of water delivered to customers costs no more than it has to.

Water is our most important natural resource, but until the last two or three decades, it was generally taken for granted by most customers. Now, as a result of growing environmental awareness and increases in the cost of water service, consumers are beginning to look at water, and at water utilities in general, from a different perspective.

Why has the cost of water increased? A primary reason is the added cost of complying with the Safe Drinking Water Act (SDWA) and other environmental regulations. Drinking water is being treated and tested as never before. Increased health-related concerns and rapid advances in technology continue to serve as catalysts to improve the quality of treatment and monitoring performed by water utilities, resulting in increased capital and operating costs.

In general, major projects undertaken by a water utility that could adversely impact the environment must undergo regulatory and public scrutiny. If a utility does not provide sufficient justification for constructing a new dam, installing a large pipeline, putting up a water storage tank, or building a pumping station, the utility could be denied permission to do so. All of these demands put pressure on the utility and on water system operators to make sure that every gallon of water delivered to customers costs no more than it has to; meets state and federal health requirements; is palatable; and is used wisely by the public, business, and industry.

WATER USE

Public water supply uses can be grouped into three categories: domestic, industrial, and public.

Domestic Use

Domestic water use is considered to be water that is supplied to residential areas, commercial districts, and institutional facilities.

- *Residential.* Water used by residential households includes both interior uses (toilets, showers, clothes washers, faucets, etc.) and exterior uses (car washing, lawn watering, etc.). The amount of water used by households varies with factors such as the age and number of occupants in a household, income level, and geographic location. Typical data for interior water use are presented in Figure 5–1. Outdoor water use is strongly influenced by the annual weather patterns; hot, dry climates having a significantly higher quantity of use than colder, wetter climates. Table 5–1 shows an analysis of water use by a typical family of four persons living in a single-family house.

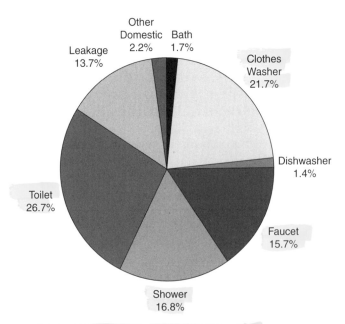

FIGURE 5–1 Indoor per capita use percentage by fixture

- *Commercial.* Water use for commercial facilities can vary widely depending on the type of activity (e.g., office as compared to a restaurant). In addition to water used for drinking and sanitary purposes by employees and customers, many commercial users also have special water needs, such as for cooling, humidifying, washing, ice making, vegetable and produce watering, ornamental fountains, and landscape irrigation.

- *Institutional.* Water used by facilities such as hospitals and schools is usually based on the size of the facility and the type of housing provided (e.g., per bed or per student). Water use by schools will be highly dependent on whether the students are housed on campus or are day students.

TABLE 5–1 Typical residential end uses of water by a family of four[*]

Fixture/End Use	Average gallons per capita per day	Average liters per capita per day	Indoor use, %	Total use, %
Toilet	18.5	70	30.9	10.8
Clothes washer	15	56.8	25.1	8.7
Shower	11.6	43.9	19.4	6.8
Faucet	10.9	41.3	18.2	6.3
Other domestic	1.6	6.1	2.7	0.9
Bathtub	1.2	4.5	2.0	0.7
Dishwasher	1	3.8	1.7	0.6
Indoor Total	**59.8**	**226.4**	**100.0**	**34.8**
Leakage	9.5	36	NA	5.5
Unknown	1.7	6.4	NA	1.0
Outdoor	100.8	381.5	NA	58.7
TOTAL	**171.8**	**650.3**	**NA**	**100.0**

[*]Data collected from the following cities: Boulder, Colo.; Denver, Colo.; Eugene, Ore.; Seattle, Wash.; San Diego, Calif.; Tampa, Fla.; Phoenix, Ariz.; Tempe, Ariz.; Scottsdale, Ariz.; Cambridge, Ont., Canada; Waterloo, Ont., Canada; Las Virgenes, Calif.; Walnut Valley, Calif.; and Lompoc, Calif. (Adapted from AwwaRF 1999).

Industrial Use

Water use by industries varies widely. It depends on the type of industry, water cost, wastewater disposal practices, types of processes and equipment, and local water conservation and reuse practices. In general, industries that use large quantities of water are located in communities where water quality is good and the cost is reasonable.

Historically, major industrial water users (such as the steel, petroleum products, pulp and paper, and power industries) have provided their own water supplies. Smaller industries and industries with low water usage generally purchase water from public systems.

Public Use

Municipalities and other public entities provide public services that require varying amounts of water. Some typical public uses are

- public parks, golf courses, swimming pools, and other recreational areas;
- municipal buildings;
- fire fighting; and
- public works uses such as street cleaning, sewer flushing, and water system flushing.

It should be noted that although the total annual volume of water required for fire fighting is typically small, the rate of flow required during a fire can be very large. A large fire in a small community can put a significant strain on a water system. For example, a community that uses an average of 1 mgd (4 ML/d) or 694 gpm (2,637 L/min) might reasonably expect a fire flow demand of 3,000 gpm (11,400 L/min) for up to 3 hours. The rate of flow for fire fighting in this case is more than four times the average daily flow, and it will likely be required from a few water mains in proximity to the fire.

Variations in Water Use

Water use for a municipality or community can vary due to a number of factors, including

- time of day and day of the week;
- climate and season of the year;
- type of community (residential or industrial) and the economy of the area;
- presence or absence of customer meters;
- dependability and quality of the water;

- connection to a sewer system or to individual onsite wastewater treatment and disposal system;
- condition of the water system (leakage and losses); and
- water conservation/demand management.

Time of day and day of week

The time of day and the day of the week can have a profound effect on water use. On a typical day in most communities, water use is lowest at night (11 p.m. to 5 a.m.) when most people are asleep. Water use rises rapidly in the morning (5 a.m. to 11 a.m.) followed by moderate usage through midday (11 a.m. to 6 p.m.). Usage then increases in the evening (6 p.m. to 10 p.m.) and drops rather quickly around 10:00 p.m. A diurnal curve showing the hourly rate of water use for a community on a typical day is shown in Figure 5–2.

Total water use for a community typically varies depending on the day of the week, and the day-to-day patterns vary depending on the habits of the community. Some water systems have significant increases in water use on Monday because it

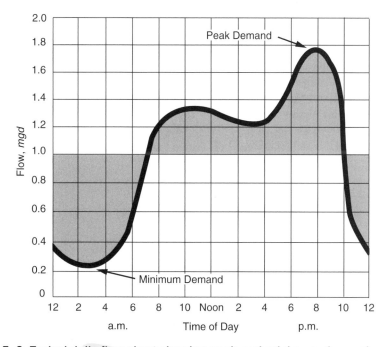

FIGURE 5–2 Typical daily flow chart showing peak and minimum demands

is historically "wash day" for many households. Water systems supplying industries that do not operate on weekends will often have reduced water use on Saturday and Sunday.

Climate and season

Water use is typically highest during the summer months when it is hot and dry, due largely to increased need for exterior uses such as landscape irrigation. Seasonal variations are commonly observed in resort areas, small communities with college campuses, and communities with seasonal commercial or industrial activities.

Most systems have relatively low water use in winter when there is no lawn or garden sprinkling or other outside activities. However, in extremely cold weather, consumers sometimes run water faucets continuously to prevent water pipes from freezing.

Air-conditioning units and cooling towers operate by evaporating water and are used extensively by homes and large commercial and industrial facilities located in hot, dry climates. The demand for water to support air conditioners and cooling towers generally coincides with periods of highest water demand for lawn and garden sprinkling.

Type and size of community

The type of housing in the service area will affect water use. For example, areas that have individual homes on large lots with gardens and lawns will typically have a much higher water use per person than areas with multiple-family dwellings such as townhomes, condominiums, and apartment complexes. Households with automatic washing machines, dishwashers, and garbage disposals tend to use more water than households where these appliances are not installed. Economically depressed areas will generally have a lower per capita water use.

Community size typically affects the peak rate of use. Compared to larger water systems, the ratio of the peak use to the average use tends to be greater for systems serving small communities.

Metering

Most water utilities have meters installed on all water services, but some systems do not have customer meters and continue to charge customers a flat rate regardless of the quantity of water they use. It has been found that flat-rate customers may use as much as 25 percent more water than is used by customers who have to pay for the actual amount of water they use. This excess water usage can be caused by unnecessary and unrestricted sprinkling and by obvious wastage (e.g., letting a faucet run to get cold water or letting a hose run while washing a car). Another problem is that household leaks are often ignored because the wasted water costs the customer nothing.

Dependability and quality of water

Customers will generally use less water if the supply is unreliable (poor pressure or limited quantity) or if it has an unpleasant taste, odor, or color. They may also use less if it has a high mineral content.

Sewer connection

The availability of municipal sewer systems has been found to increase water use. Homes with sewer service usually have more appliances and fixtures that use water because there is no worry about overloading an onsite wastewater treatment and disposal system. The increase in water use due to sewer availability may be 50 to 100 percent.

Condition of the water system

Unaccounted-for water can generally be described as the difference between the average annual water production and the average annual metered consumption of a system. Unaccounted-for water can result from many factors, including leaks in piping, main breaks, periodic fire hydrant flushing, tank drainage for maintenance purposes, unauthorized use, unmetered services, and inaccurate or non-functioning meters. Unaccounted-for system leakage and losses may range from 10 to 12 percent of production for new distribution systems (less than 25 years old) and from 15 to 30 percent for older systems. Leakage can be caused by system age, materials of construction, and lack of system maintenance. Water mains are usually tested for water tightness when they are installed. As the water mains get older, leakage at pipe joints, valves, and connections increases. Unless periodic checks are made to locate and repair leaks, the amount of water lost daily can be significant. This lost water can place an extra strain on the ability of the utility to furnish water to customers, and it also represents a loss of revenue.

WATER CONSERVATION

There is no universally accepted definition of *water conservation*. This book considers water conservation to be any beneficial reduction in water use or in water losses. The last three decades have seen a steady progression in the acceptance of water conservation in the United States. Water utilities in water-short areas have been leaders in conservation efforts. For utilities in areas of prolonged drought, the benefits of water use reduction are obvious. The benefits are less obvious in an area that has adequate rainfall, a relatively stable population, and a source with an adequate safe yield. The total beneficial effects (benefits) of the reduction in water use or water losses resulting from implementation of a conservation program should be greater than the adverse effects (costs).

Potential Benefits of Water Conservation

The potential benefits of water conservation include

- *Reduced demand on the supply source.* A reduction in water use, whether from a surface water or groundwater source, can allow a larger population to be served by the same size source. This is particularly relevant for aquifers that are becoming depleted and surface water sources that serve the increasing demands of growing communities. Reductions in demand can also extend supplies during an emergency.

- *Reduction of water and wastewater flow.* Reducing water use can result in reductions in water and wastewater flows, which in turn can reduce a utility's power costs for water/wastewater pumping and treatment. Reduced water and wastewater flows can also extend the capacity of treatment, pumping, and piping, thereby deferring, eliminating, or downsizing new facilities.

- *Reduced costs for utility and customer.* A reduction in water use can provide energy savings for the water utility. Pumping costs can be reduced, as can the costs for power and chemicals required for all stages of treatment. In addition, when heated water is conserved, energy costs will be reduced in homes, businesses, and industry.

- *Protection of the environment.* Reducing the supply required from a stream or surface water impoundment can benefit the plants and animals that depend on it. This aspect of water conservation is receiving increased attention from environmental organizations and governmental agencies.

Potential Problems With Water Conservation

Although the benefits of water conservation can be significant, there are some potential negative aspects that must also be considered. These include:

- *Utility and customer program costs.* The cost for implementing a conservation program will likely be borne by the water utility and the water utility's customers. Costs for programs can vary depending on the implementation method, size of the program, and the extent of the evaluation planned (i.e., surveys, billing data reviews, water audits, etc.). These short-term and long-term costs should be quantified to the extent possible for each component of the water conservation program.

- *Loss of revenue for the utility.* When a utility implements a water conservation program and does not increase water rates, it will receive less income because of reduced water sales. There will be some offsetting savings to the utility due to lower energy and chemical costs, but the revenue loss can still be substantial. Often the only way to compensate for this loss in revenue is to raise water rates. A water system manager must realize before starting a conservation program that revenue will decrease. The manager must take steps to ensure that adequate revenue will be available to meet financial obligations, such as bond payments. If a utility must suddenly implement water conservation because of a water shortage, the unplanned loss of revenue may be quite serious because it is difficult to raise rates on short notice. In other words, it is better to plan in advance than to wait until it happens.

- *Possible delay in developing additional source capacity.* When a water crisis is alleviated through conservation, the public may find it hard to understand why there is still a need for long-range water resource development projects. Lack of public support could then delay (or eliminate from further consideration) development of a new reservoir, wellfield, or other new water source that is needed. This delay can, in turn, increase the cost of the project, as well as worsen the water crisis if there is a drought year before the new facilities can be constructed.

- *Possible stimulation of water service growth.* The water saved by a conservation program will allow more people to be served by the amount of water available. This can act as a stimulant for growth. As long as water still appears to be available for use, additional customers may continue to be connected to the system. This action may not be in the best interests of the water system or community, at least until a more ample supply can be obtained.

- *Difficulty in dealing with drought conditions.* When a drought occurs after a utility has a conservation program in effect, the situation can become very difficult. It is sometimes hard to explain why it is necessary to conserve even further. This emphasizes the need for water supply planning as an integral part of conservation planning. The utility must insist that looking to the future water supply needs of a community is as important as any other aspect of a conservation program.

Supply Management Techniques

In conjunction with any water conservation program, a utility should first examine its own practices in properly managing the available supply of water. This process is called supply management. Some features of supply management are

- *Careful management of all resources.* Maintaining an adequate source of supply should be part of both a long-range (25 years or more) and short-range (5 years) plan. The plan should be in writing and be made available to all local interest groups for comment and review.

- *Analysis of water use data.* A database on water use should be developed, including, but not limited to, data on average daily production, peak demand, and geographical and seasonal water use patterns. The complexity of this database should grow with utility size so that any unexpected change can be analyzed for its impact on total water use.

- *Complete source and customer metering.* All sources of supply and customer services should be metered. Complete metering is necessary for comparing the amount of water used by customers against the amount pumped to the system.

- *Reduction of unaccounted-for water.* The difference between the amount of water pumped to the system and the amount metered to customers (or otherwise accounted-for) is called unaccounted-for water. Unaccounted-for water is generally water that is wasted through leaks or unauthorized use. State utility commissions usually have formulas that can be used to calculate unaccounted-for water. Unaccounted-for system leakage and losses may range from 10 to 12 percent of production for new distribution systems (less than 25 years old) and from 15 to 30 percent for older systems. If the amount of unaccounted-for water appears to be substantial, a system-wide leak survey should be conducted. In addition, leak awareness for field personnel can be promoted by a program of listening for leaks on hydrants, services, and meters.

Demand Management Techniques

In conjunction with the program to manage the available supply, a utility must develop and implement demand management programs to encourage the public to reduce water usage. Demand management can consist of the following:

- public education;
- distribution of water-saving devices;
- management of water use demands;
- modification of the water rate structure;
- use of water-saving plumbing fixtures;
- promotion of low-water-use gardening and agricultural practices; and
- promotion of water conservation by businesses and industries.

Public education

Educating the public is usually a key component of a water conservation program. If water rates are low or moderate, customers may need considerable incentive to participate in a water conservation program. Printed materials and suggested programs are available from the American Water Works Association (AWWA), state water organizations, state agencies, and the US Environmental Protection Agency (USEPA), as well as environmental and conservation organizations. An effective way of reaching and informing the public about the conservation program is by offering speakers, literature, and videos to local schools, service clubs, and civic groups.

Customers can also be educated directly by the use of bill stuffers and conservation notes. Direct assistance in detecting leaks or developing water use audits should be offered to customers. Newspapers, radio, and television stations should also be supplied with public service announcements (PSAs) and press releases explaining the program. A utility's Web site can also be an effective way of explaining the program to the public.

Water-saving devices

Many water utilities offer water-saving kits to residential customers. These kits reduce water use by altering the flow of water through regular plumbing fixtures. A typical kit includes faucet aerators to decrease faucet flow, a low-flow showerhead or flow restrictor, and a toilet flapper to reduce leakage. Some utilities offer their customers rebates for replacing older-model toilets with low-flow models. The cost of these kits can be fully paid by the customer, partially paid by the customer, or fully funded by the utility. State regulatory agencies have mandated the use of these kits in many areas and have stipulated that the cost be shared by the customer and utility.

Managing water use demands

Some sections of a water system may experience water shortage as a result of inadequate distribution system capacity. If this occurs, the utility may gain some relief by educating the public about the problem and encouraging them to use water during off-peak hours. Mandating that water for lawn watering or car washing be used only on alternating days is a common summer water use restriction. These restrictions can be either mandatory or voluntary.

Rate structure modification

Rate structure changes are gaining in popularity as a way to encourage water conservation. There are a variety of choices, and information on them can be obtained from AWWA and public utility regulatory agencies.

Water-saving plumbing fixtures

The Energy Policy Act of 1992 established water conservation standards for the manufacture of four types of plumbing fixtures: toilets, kitchen and lavatory faucets, showerheads, and urinals. With limited exceptions, the standards apply to all models of the fixtures manufactured after Jan. 1, 1994. Approximately 16 states and 6 localities had water-efficient standards for at least two of the plumbing fixtures regulated under the Energy Policy Act before the national standards took effect in 1994. Studies have shown that, compared to their less efficient counterparts, low-flow fixtures conserve water, particularly in the case of toilets.

Low-water-use landscaping practices

The use of landscaping requiring very low water use is called Xeriscaping (Figure 5–3). It is being encouraged for home and business landscaping in semi-arid and arid areas as a means of conserving irrigation water. There are excellent publications on this subject (see Suggested Supplementary Readings at the end of this chapter). The use of drought-tolerant landscaping also has value in areas where there are seasonal shortages of water.

Business and industry conservation

Utilities can often achieve great savings in water use by working with business and industry. Increasing water rates is a very strong motivation for these groups. However, careful consideration of how water is used or wasted in a manufacturing plant can also lead to significant reductions. In some instances, installing smaller, more sensitive meters in businesses and industries can generate considerable revenue by more accurately recording low flows and can serve as a stimulus to water conservation.

Droughts

One of the most serious threats to the ability of a water utility to meet the demands of its customers is a drought. The actions required to meet a drought emergency are to locate an additional supply, reduce demands, or both.

Each water system should have an emergency response plan to address how water will be provided under all conceivable disasters. Although a drought can be very serious, immediate response is not usually necessary. There is usually a period

Source: Doug Hanford, Hanford Company Landscape Design; John Nelson, North Marin Water District; Ali Davidson, Sonoma County Water Agency.

FIGURE 5–3 Typical water-efficient landscaping

of weeks or even months when it becomes obvious that source supplies are dwindling. Therefore, finding additional sources of water and reducing water use should not be done during an acute crisis.

Emergency procedures to reduce water use may be similar to routine water conservation, but the actions required will be more severe when the situation is critical. For instance, some communities issue warnings and fines for unauthorized uses, such as washing a car or watering the lawn during an acute water shortage.

WATER RIGHTS

From the beginning of recorded history, people have recognized the value of water and argued over its ownership. In the United States, the issue of water rights is one that is growing in importance and intensity. There are many arguments over who owns a source of water and who gets to use it. The arguments may be between individuals, between communities, between states, between states and the federal government, and between countries.

Allocation of Surface Water

The two basic systems for the allocation of water from surface lakes and streams in the United States are

- riparian doctrine, which is commonly used in the water-rich eastern part of the country, and
- appropriation doctrine, which is used in the more arid western states.

Riparian doctrine

The riparian doctrine is sometimes called the "rule of reasonable sharing." The basic theory in all states that follow this doctrine is that there should be equal sharing among those who own the land abutting a body of water. However, there are substantial differences in how the law is applied.

The basic principle is sharing, rather than a right to a specific amount of water or a certain rate of flow. In general, the riparian property owner can use as much water as desired for any reasonable purpose, as long as this use does not interfere with the reasonable use by other riparian property owners.

Thus, the presence of a water shortage means that all riparian property owners suffer equally and each must accept a reduction in supply. The rights of an owner of land abutting a water source are not affected by how long the land has been owned or by how much water the owner has used in the past.

Riparian rights represent a common-law doctrine. This means that they are a part of a large body of civil law that, for the most part, was made by judges in court decisions in individual cases, rather than statutory law enacted by a legislative body.

Because the possession of rights arises from ownership of land abutting a water body, all of the owners are treated as equals by the courts. Conflicts are then usually resolved by the court, which determines what is reasonable use. This is not clearly defined and is not an absolute. Many factors and values are considered, including

- purpose of the use,
- its suitability to the water body,

- its economic or social value,
- the amount of harm caused by the use,
- the amount of harm avoided by changing either party's use, and
- the protection of existing values.

The growth of water use in riparian-doctrine states has led to more frequent conflicts created by water shortages. A number of these states have tried to remedy weaknesses in the doctrine by enacting statutes that require permits to be obtained from a state agency. These permits vary widely in the restrictions they apply and the requirements they place on the riparian.

This move to the issuance of permits brings the states closer to the appropriation doctrine. The permit systems are criticized by some and considered unnecessary by others. They have not undergone serious challenges in the courts, so their eventual success is not guaranteed. The trend toward permit systems, however, is continuing.

Appropriation doctrine

The appropriation doctrine concept started with the forty-niners in the gold fields of California. When there was too little water for all the mining operations, the principle applied was "first in time, first in right." The principle was given legal recognition by the courts and later made into law by western state legislatures. Currently, the most important water use in the West is for irrigation, so to a great degree, the appropriation doctrine is irrigation law.

The appropriation doctrine rests on two basic principles: priority in time and beneficial use.

Priority in time. When streamflow is less than demand, use is prioritized based on who has been using the water for the longest period of time. The most recent uses are discontinued in order to provide water for the earlier uses. There is no sharing of suffering, which is a hallmark of the riparian doctrine.

Beneficial use. Beneficial use is, in many ways, quite the opposite of riparian doctrine. There is no water right based on land ownership alone. Instead, water rights are acquired by proving that water is being used beneficially. A user who has been appropriated water continues to be entitled to it only when it can be used beneficially. Waste is therefore theoretically prohibited, and any available water beyond the amount that can be used by one appropriator is available to others. In addition, nonuse of the water for a long period may result in loss of the water right by forfeiture or abandonment.

Beneficial use is seldom defined precisely. There are two different but related aspects: the type of use (such as irrigation, mining, or municipal use) and efficiency. Most use is judged beneficial, and the majority of court cases have been about inefficient or wasteful uses.

Legal complications.   When we consider disputes over real estate, rights are reasonably clear. People respect boundaries in most cases, and lawsuits are a suitable means of settling the few disputes that do occur. Water rights are different. Water is a shared resource, making water rights highly interdependent and relative. Boundaries are not obvious and are constantly changing.

With the appropriation doctrine, the assignment of a right at any particular time depends on streamflow, the number of prior existing rights, and the amount of water needed by the person or entity with the prior rights. For many western streams, the exercise of rights might have to be adjusted daily in times of heavy use, such as in summer. Irrigation uses, for example, make quick adjustments imperative, and the nature of the stream and river systems can complicate the issue.

Allocation of Groundwater
The following four water rights systems are used for groundwater:

1. absolute ownership,
2. reasonable use,
3. correlative rights, and
4. appropriation-permit systems.

Absolute ownership
The absolute ownership system is based on the principle that the owner of the land owns everything beneath that land to the center of the earth. A better understanding of the nature of groundwater makes it impossible to apply this ownership literally. For all practical purposes, the system is a rule of capture. The landowner can use all the water that can be "captured" from beneath the owner's land.

There are almost no restrictions applied to this rule. The water can be used for the owner's purposes both on and off the land, and it can be sold to others. There is no liability if pumping reduces a neighbor's supply or even dries up the neighbor's well. Some interpretations even say that water can be wasted as long as it is not done maliciously.

Reasonable use

As is true with the rule of absolute ownership, the rule of reasonable use holds that groundwater rights are part of land ownership. The owner has the right to pump and use groundwater. However, if this use interferes with a neighbor's use, it may continue only if it is reasonable. Conversely, an owner is liable if unreasonable use causes harm to others. This amounts to a *qualified right* rather than an *absolute right* to use groundwater.

It is obvious that the determination of what is reasonable is the important factor in the rule. Reasonable use is much easier to determine for groundwater than for surface water under the riparian doctrine. In general, any use of water that is not wasteful for a purpose associated with the land from which the water is drawn (an overlying use) is reasonable. Conversely, any use off the property may be considered unreasonable if it interferes with the use of the groundwater sources by others.

The overlying use criterion, however, does not resolve disputes if all parties to the dispute are using the water for overlying purposes. In this case, all uses are reasonable, all can continue, and "reasonable" use becomes the rule of capture—in other words, the owner with the biggest pump gets the water. On the other hand, because a nonoverlying use is considered unreasonable if it interferes with an overlying use, such uses are forbidden no matter how beneficial.

Correlative rights

The rule of correlative rights holds that the overlying use rule is not absolute but is related to the rights of other overlying users. This rule is used when there is not enough water to satisfy all overlying uses. In this case, the rule requires sharing. This rule has been applied by prorating the available water supply according to the size of the overlying land parcel.

Appropriation–permit system

The appropriation–permit system is sometimes called a groundwater appropriation system; in reality, it is more of a permit system. The most important issue here is the rule of priority (water rights are based on who has used the water for the longest period of time). Priority is all-important in the appropriation doctrine as applied to surface water because the variation in streamflows requires frequent adjustment of withdrawals. However, groundwater in the aquifer is stored to a certain extent, and this storage buffers the supply so that frequent adjustment is not necessary. This means that priority, as applied to groundwater, mainly involves limiting the number of permits to prevent overuse of the aquifer.

The permit system thus amounts to groundwater management and administrative regulation. By placing limitations on pumping rates, wellfield placement, and well construction standards and by refusing permits when necessary, for example, the administrating agency manages groundwater. Permit systems vary widely. The only generalization that can be made is that permits can be more relaxed if adequate water is available and more stringent if it is not.

Summary of Water Rights

There is a great variety in how rights are interpreted and how water rights are managed in US states and territories. The evolution of water resources management is more complete in the West, where water is frequently in short supply, than in the East, where supplies have been more plentiful. Management beyond the basic principles described here varies from state to state. The water utility operator should contact the state agency responsible for water resource management and obtain copies of applicable regulations.

SELECTED SUPPLEMENTARY READINGS

Back to Basics Guide to Water Conservation. 1991. Denver, Colo.: American Water Works Association.

Ball, K. 1990. *Xeriscape Programs for Water Utilities.* Denver, Colo.: American Water Works Association.

Bowen, P.T., J.F. Harp, J.W. Baxter, and R.D. Shull. 1993. *Residential Water Use Patterns.* Denver, Colo.: Awwa Research Foundation and American Water Works Association.

Driscoll, F.G. 1986. *Groundwater and Wells.* St. Paul, Minn.: Johnson Filtration Systems, Inc.

Drought Management Planning. 1992. Denver, Colo.: American Water Works Association.

Evaluating Urban Water Conservation Programs: A Procedures Manual. 1993. Denver, Colo.: American Water Works Association.

Federal Environmental Law Constraints on Drinking Water Supply Development. 1992. Denver, Colo.: American Water Works Association.

Gilbert, J.B., W.J. Bishop, and J.A. Weber. 1990. Reducing Water Demand During Drought Years. *Jour. AWWA,* 82(5):34.

Helping Businesses Manage Water Use. 1993. Denver, Colo.: American Water Works Association.

Kollar, K.L., and P. MacAuley. 1980. Water Requirements for Industrial Development. *Jour. AWWA,* 72(2):1.

Macy, P.P., and W.O. Maddaus. 1989. Cost-Benefit Analysis of Conservation Programs. *Jour. AWWA,* 81(3):43.

Maddaus, W.O. 1987. *Water Conservation.* Denver, Colo.: American Water Works Association.

Mayer, P.W. et al. 1999. *Residential End Uses of Water.* Denver, Colo.: Awwa Research Foundation and American Water Works Association.

Solley, W.B., R.R. Pierce, and H.A. Perlman. 1993. *Estimated Use of Water in the United States in 1990.* US Geological Survey Circular 1081. Washington, D.C.: US Government Printing Office.

van der Luden, F., F.L. Troise, and D.K. Todd. 1990. *The Water Encyclopedia, 2nd ed.* Chelsea, Mich.: Lewis Publishers.

The Water Conservation Manager's Guide to Residential Retrofit. 1993. Denver, Colo.: American Water Works Association.

Wright, K. 1990. *Water Rights in the Fifty States and Territories.* Denver, Colo.: American Water Works Association.

Wright, K. 1998. *Water Rights of the Eastern United States.* Denver, Colo.: American Water Works Association.

6

Water Quality

It is important that all public water systems serve water of the best possible quality to their customers. If the quality is poor, customers will generally reduce consumption, and if it is very bad, they will look elsewhere for water.

If customers do obtain drinking water from another source, health officials fear that the substitute could be unsafe, especially if it comes from an unprotected or contaminated source. The substitute, bottled water, for example, might also be very expensive. It is undesirable for the customer to lose confidence in the water utility and the water industry. The utility may then find it difficult to obtain approval for rate increases and hard to rally public support for improvements such as developing new water sources, upgrading treatment, and improving the distribution system.

A loss of confidence in the utility on the part of the public is difficult to overcome. It can be overcome, however, if the utility, the regulator, environmental groups, and the media work together to reassure the public of the safety of the product. Water utility operators must take the lead in this cooperative effort by ensuring that the goals of potability and palatability are met. The actions of the utility must be open to the public, and the customers should be kept informed through bill stuffers and public service announcements. The utility may also sponsor special information programs in conjunction with publicizing National Drinking Water Week.

WATER QUALITY CHARACTERISTICS

Water quality characteristics fall into the following four broad categories:

1. physical,
2. chemical,
3. biological, and
4. radiological.

The quality of water is based, to a great extent, on the concentration of the constituents that are present. The smallest unit of water, the water molecule (H_2O), contains two atoms of hydrogen (H) and one atom of oxygen (O). Anything present in the water other than water molecules may be considered a constituent. In the natural environment, there is no such thing as pure water. During its passage, water acquires dissolved and suspended constituents that may not be desirable for its potable use. Treatment is required if the levels of undesirable constituents, termed either impurities or contaminants, are above their allowable levels based on either health or aesthetic concerns. Even rain and snow may contain impurities. The type and quantity of constituents in water also dictate the level and type of treatment required to make the water potable.

This is even true of distilled water, which often has traces of chemicals that are not completely removed in the distillation process. In fact, industries that require very pure water, such as the electronic chip industry, use elaborate treatment facilities to produce ultrapure water that is almost completely free of impurities. Because water is capable of dissolving trace amounts of almost anything, highly treated water must be used immediately, rather than being stored.

Water Contaminants

It is now common practice for the undesired constituents in water to be called contaminants. Many water constituents are harmless, and some are even beneficial. Examples of beneficial constituents include fluoride and calcium in acceptable concentrations.

Measuring contaminant levels

The concentration of a particular constituent in water is usually very small and is measured in milligrams per liter (mg/L). This means that the quantity of a constituent in a standard volume (a liter) of water is measured by its weight (in milligrams). A concentration of 1 mg/L of magnesium in water would be about the same as 0.00013 ounces of magnesium in each gallon of water. More and more constituents, especially organic contaminants, in water are being regulated at the parts-per-billion and some even at parts-per-trillion levels.

In water, concentrations expressed as milligrams per liter, within the range of 0–2,000 mg/L (dilute solution), are roughly equivalent to concentrations expressed as parts per million (ppm). For example, 12 mg/L of calcium in water is roughly the same as 12 ppm calcium in water.

Mineral concentrations

The mineral content of any water consists of individual chemicals, such as calcium, magnesium, sodium, iron, manganese, bicarbonate, carbonate, sulfate, and chloride. Generally, in the absence of individual chemical levels, an aggregate parameter, namely, total dissolved solids, represents the mineral content of the water. The examples given in Table 6–1 provide a general idea of the relative magnitude of mineral concentrations in various sources of water.

In general, river water has a dissolved-minerals concentration of less than 500 mg/L, although some rivers may have concentrations of 2,000 mg/L or more. Mineral concentrations in groundwater can vary from several hundred to more than 10,000 mg/L.

TABLE 6–1 Typical surface water mineral concentrations

Source of Water	Total Dissolved Minerals, *mg/L*
Distilled	<1
Rain	10
Lake Tahoe	70
Suwannee River	150
Lake Michigan	170
Missouri River	360
Pecos River	2,600
Ocean	35,000
Brine well	125,000
Dead Sea	250,000

Physical and Other Characteristics

The physical properties of water that are important in water treatment include

- turbidity,
- alkalinity,
- color,
- temperature,
- hardness,
- tastes and odors,
- dissolved solids, and
- electrical conductivity.

Turbidity

Turbidity, or cloudiness in water, is generally caused by the suspended and colloidal matter consisting of finely divided solids that are larger than molecules. The solids can be of inorganic origin and include clay, silt, and asbestos fibers, as well as living and dead organic matter such as algae, bacteria, and other microorganisms.

When a beam of light passes through turbid water, some of the light reflects off the suspended particles. Measurements of the intensity of this light indicate the amount of turbidity present. Turbidity is expressed in terms of nephelometric turbidity units (ntu).

Although the presence of turbidity in drinking water is an aesthetic concern, it is also a health concern. The particulates may themselves be toxic or may have adsorbed toxic material. There is a particular concern that harmful microorganisms adsorbed to the particles will be shielded against disinfectants and will thus remain infective.

Because of the natural filtering effect of soils, groundwater turbidity is often less than 1 ntu; however, the presence of iron and manganese may increase the turbidity levels upon extraction of water. Surface water turbidities vary widely from less than 1 ntu to more than 1,000 ntu (generally associated with storm events).

Alkalinity

In simple words, alkalinity is water's ability to neutralize acids. Alkalinity is a function of the carbonate, bicarbonate, and hydroxide content of the water. Water with higher alkalinity has higher buffering capacity, that is, the water can maintain a steady pH upon addition of acid. At low alkalinity levels, even a small quantity of acid can decrease the pH dramatically. Also, hard waters generally have high alkalinity. Alkalinity in source waters is influenced by minerals and salts, as well as plant uptake and metabolism, and industrial wastewater discharges. Alkalinity of water is measured by adding acid to a sample and is expressed as milligrams per liter as calcium carbonate (mg/L as $CaCO_3$).

Alkalinity plays a very important role in the treatment of water. Some chemicals used for coagulation of suspended matter consume alkalinity and therefore impact the water's pH. Sometimes additional alkalinity is added so that sufficient pH is maintained in the treated water. Alkalinity, along with other water quality parameters, also plays an important role in the corrosion control of water distribution systems.

Color

Color in raw water is primarily a problem for surface waters. It usually indicates the presence of decomposed organic material such as leaves, roots, or plant remains. It may also be due to a high concentration of inorganic chemicals or to upstream domestic or industrial wastewater discharges. Color in water can sometimes indicate pollution that might be harmful.

Generally, color in water is reported either as "true color" or "apparent color," depending on the absence or presence of suspended matter, respectively, in the water sample. Color is measured by comparing the color of a sample with the color of a standard chemical (chloroplatinate) solution. The units of measure are color units (cu). A color of less than 15 cu usually passes unnoticed, whereas a color of 100 cu has the appearance of light tea. Highly colored water is objectionable for most industrial uses; from an aesthetic standpoint, it is unsuitable for drinking water. Figure 6–1 shows a colorimeter used to measure color.

Temperature

Water temperature, which impacts the rates of chemical reactions, is important in water treatment. For example, chemicals used for treatment are dissolved more easily in warm water and suspended particles will also settle out more quickly. However, warmer temperatures encourage the growth of various forms of plant life in water.

From the consumer's standpoint, cold water is preferred because it tastes better. When industries use water for cooling and process-manufacturing, they generally prefer cold water.

The temperature of water in lakes and reservoirs generally varies with depth. The heavier cold water will normally be at the bottom, with warmer water near the surface. However, as air temperatures become colder in the fall, the surface water cools and eventually becomes slightly heavier than the water below. At that point, the lake "turns over" as the cold surface water sinks to the bottom. The

Courtesy of Fisher Scientific

FIGURE 6-1 Colorimeter used in treatment plant lab

turbulence created by a lake turnover can disperse decomposed bottom deposits throughout the reservoir. This can create a very unpleasant odor in the water and can cause quality and treatment problems for several days or weeks.

The reverse of this process usually occurs in the spring. By knowing the water temperature at various levels in a reservoir, the operator is more likely to antici-pate turnover and select the level of withdrawal that will produce the best-quality water. Methods of preventing lake stratification are discussed in another book in this series, *Water Treatment*.

Temperature is measured on either of two scales: Fahrenheit or Celsius. The Fahrenheit scale is primarily used in the United States. The Celsius scale is used by most other countries and in scientific work. Relationships between the two scales are as follows:

Fahrenheit (F): Freezing point = 32°F
  Boiling point = 212°F

$°F = {}^9/5 (°C) + 32$
Celsius (C): Freezing point = 0°C
  Boiling point = 100°C
$°C = {}^5/9 (°F) - 32$

Hardness

A "hard" water contains significant amounts of calcium, magnesium, and other minerals. Hard water can be a problem in water supply and treatment because, like water with a high pH, it can cause scale to form in pipes and meters. Hardness in water can vary from values with single digits to those in the hundreds.

If water is hot, as in boilers and hot-water lines, the scale forms much faster. One millimeter (0.04 in.) of deposited scale can increase the cost of heating hot water by more than 10 percent. If water from a public water system is very hard, many customers install individual home water softeners.

Hard water may also have an objectionable taste and it requires more soap when used for washing. A standard laboratory test for hardness determines the amount of both calcium and magnesium in the water, but for convenience, the results are expressed in milligrams per liter as $CaCO_3$. Table 6–2 summarizes typical degrees of hardness and the corresponding concentrations.

Tastes and odors

Tastes and odors in water can be caused by a wide variety of materials including algae, decaying organic matter, industrial and domestic wastes, minerals, and dissolved gases. Highly mineralized waters have a saline, medicinal, or metallic taste. On the other hand, small amounts of minerals and dissolved gases can give

TABLE 6–2 Hardness concentrations and typical corresponding designations

Common Designation	Hardness, *mg/L as CaCO₃*
Soft	0–60
Moderately hard	61–120
Hard	121–180
Very hard	Greater than 180

water a pleasant taste. Tastes and odors become more noticeable as the water temperature increases.

Although the senses of taste and smell are closely related, the sense of smell is far more discriminating. Therefore, in water treatment, usually only odor is measured. A trained person who smells a series of diluted water samples measures the intensity of odor. The person begins the test by smelling a sample of specially prepared, odor-free water and continues by smelling samples that contain increasing concentrations of the water being tested. This continues until an odor is detected. The minimum odor that can be detected is called the threshold odor. The particular dilution of that sample is called the threshold odor number (TON). The TON test is conducted on raw water to determine the degree of treatment required. The test is also regularly conducted on finished water to ensure that adequate treatment is being provided. The TON in the distributed water should be less than 3. Different treatment strategies are adopted depending on the source of taste- and odor-causing compounds. For example, earthy and musty odor typically caused by the presence of algae in the source water can be reduced by the use of activated carbon.

Dissolved solids

Because of its remarkable dissolving properties, water dissolves minerals from the soil and rock materials that it contacts. Table 6–3 demonstrates the wide variation in water quality that occurs in water from four different sources.

Water can at times contain many toxic dissolved minerals, including arsenic, barium, cadmium, chromium, lead, mercury, selenium, and silver. Other dissolved minerals, such as dissolved iron and manganese, can cause aesthetic problems, for example, turning water brown or black when the chemicals are oxidized.

The total quantity of dissolved solids in water is a general indicator of its acceptability for drinking and agricultural and industrial uses. Water with a high concentration of dissolved solids can create tastes, odors, hardness, corrosion, and scaling problems. In addition, high concentrations of dissolved solids have a laxative effect on most people. For these reasons, a secondary standard with a total dissolved solids (TDS) limit of 500 mg/L is recommended for drinking water.

Dissolved solids are measured by filtering a known volume of sample and then evaporating the filtered water to dryness. The residue that remains is weighed, and the results are recorded in milligrams per liter as filterable residue, commonly known as TDS. This test is called the filterable residue test.

Industrial users usually require water with a relatively low concentration of dissolved solids in order to prevent corrosion and boiler scale. If the water is to be incorporated into a product, the level must be quite low. On the other hand, certain irrigated crops can tolerate mineralized water at a concentration as high as 2,000 mg/L.

TABLE 6-3 Chemical quality comparison of four water sources

Chemical	Concentrations of Water Contaminants, *mg/L*			
	River*	Well†	Canal‡	Saline Lake§
Silica (SiO_2)	5.4	41	6.6	11
Iron (Fe)	0.11	0.04	0.11	0.10
Calcium (Ca)	9.6	50	83	2.9
Magnesium (Mg)	2.4	4.8	6.7	9.5
Sodium (Na)	4.2	10	12	8,690
Potassium (K)	1.1	5.1	1.2	138
Carbonate (CO_3)	0	0	0	3,010
Bicarbonate (HCO_3)	26	172	263	3,600
Sulfate (SO_4)	12	8.0	5.4	10,500
Chloride (Cl)	5.0	5.0	20	668
Fluoride (F)	0.1	0.4	0.2	—
Nitrate (NO_3)	3.2	20	1.3	5.8
Total dissolved solids	64	250	310	25,000

*Stream in Connecticut.
†Logan County, Colo.
‡Drainage from the Everglades in Florida.
§North-central North Dakota.

Electrical conductivity

A common way to obtain a quick estimate of the concentration of TDS in water is to measure the electrical conductivity (EC) of the water. Theoretically, water free of any contaminants will not conduct electricity. However, most natural substances dissolved in water allow water to conduct electricity—the greater the concentration, the greater the electrical conductivity.

The instrument used to determine EC actually measures the electrical resistance of the water between two electrodes spaced a known distance apart. The conductivity instrument readout is in micromhos per centimeter at 25°C, abbreviated μmhos/cm at 25°C. As a general rule, every 10 units of EC represents

6 to 7 mg/L of dissolved solids. Therefore, an EC of 1,000 suggests a dissolved solids concentration of about 600–700 mg/L. It should be noted that the relationship between EC and dissolved solids is somewhat different for every type of water.

An EC test takes only a few minutes, whereas the filterable residue test may take 2 hours to complete. The test is temperature sensitive, so it must always be conducted with the sample at 25°C. Electrical conductivity is measured by a conductivity meter like the ones shown in Figure 6–2.

Chemical Characteristics

Chemical characteristics of water fall into two categories: inorganic and organic. Organic chemicals have a basically carbon-based structure, whereas inorganic chemicals do not.

Chemical characteristics include

- pH,
- dissolved oxygen, and
- inorganic constituents.

Photo provided by YSI Incorporated

FIGURE 6–2 Typical electrical conductivity meters

pH

The term *pH* is used to express the acidic or alkaline condition of a solution. The pH scale runs from 0 to 14, with 7 being neutral. A pH less than 7 indicates an acidic water, and a pH greater than 7 indicates a basic, or alkaline, water. The normal pH range of surface water is 6.5 to 8.5; the pH of groundwater generally ranges from 6.0 to 8.5. A typical pH meter used to determine the pH of water is shown in operation in Figure 6–3.

The pH of water can have a marked effect on treatment plant equipment and processes. At a pH value less than 7, water has a greater tendency to corrode the equipment and other materials that it contacts (Figure 6–4). At a pH value greater than 7, water has a tendency to deposit scale, which is particularly noticeable in pipelines and hot-water home appliances (Figure 6–5).

The pH of water also has an important effect on treatment processes such as coagulation and disinfection because it also impacts the rates of chemical reactions. A number of water treatment chemicals (e.g., corrosion inhibitors) work within a specified pH range. Generally, a higher-than-neutral pH is desirable (for

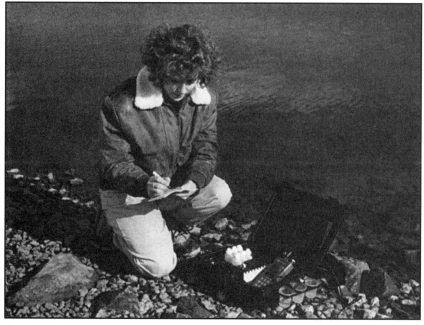

Courtesy of Fisher Scientific

FIGURE 6–3 pH testing in the field

FIGURE 6–4 Corroded pipe and appurtenance

corrosion control) for the finished water, and the pH usually needs to be adjusted if raw and treated water pH values are lower than the desired value.

Dissolved oxygen

One of the more common dissolved gases in water is oxygen. Dissolved oxygen (DO) is absolutely vital for the support of fish and other aquatic life. Oxygen can become dissolved in water in three ways:

1. The oxygen enters the water directly from the air (through natural aeration).

2. Oxygen is introduced into the water by plant life, such as algae (through photosynthesis).

3. Oxygen is introduced by mechanical equipment during treatment, such as mechanical aeration or diffused aeration.

Courtesy of Johnson Controls, Inc.

FIGURE 6–5 Pipe scaling caused by high pH values

Dissolved oxygen is almost always present to some extent in natural waters. A warm-water lake will usually contain about 5 mg/L of DO; a cold-water lake may contain 7 mg/L or more. However, if algae are present in the water, the DO level will vary greatly. During sunlight hours, algae produce oxygen, so the DO level rises. During the night, algae use the oxygen, causing the DO level to drop.

Although DO is a healthy and necessary characteristic of water, it is also an important cause of corrosion. Water containing high levels of DO will attack metallic surfaces that it contacts, such as pipes, meters, pumps, and boilers. In general, the higher the DO concentration, the more rapid the corrosion will be. DO can be measured either chemically or electrically. The measured concentration of DO is reported in milligrams per liter. A typical DO meter is shown in Figure 6–6.

Inorganic constituents

In addition to calcium, magnesium, carbonate/bicarbonate, sulfate, and chloride, water contains a number of inorganic constituents. Many of these inorganic constituents occur naturally in water, others are added (asbestos) or produced (chlorite and chlorate) during the treatment and distribution of water. Some inorganic constituents are associated with adverse health effects and include aluminum,

133

Courtesy of Fisher Scientific

FIGURE 6–6 Dissolved oxygen meter in use

antimony, arsenic, asbestos, barium, bromate, cadmium, chloride, chlorite and chlorate, chromium, copper, cyanide, fluoride, iron, lead, manganese, mercury, nickel, nitrite and nitrate, selenium, sodium, sulfates, and zinc. Many of these inorganic constituents are carcinogenic (cancer causing) (e.g., arsenic). Different methods for analyses of inorganic constituents include colorimetric, atomic absorption, inductively coupled plasma, and ion chromatography.

Organic characteristics

Organics are another category of chemical characteristics. To date, more than 1,000 organic chemicals have been identified in drinking water supplies. Organic chemicals have four general sources:

1. Plant decomposition yields materials such as tannins, lignins, and fulvic and humic materials. Surrogate parameters, such as total organic carbon (TOC) and ultraviolet (UV) absorbance, are used to quantify the natural organic matter content of water.

2. Municipal and industrial wastewater discharges may add natural and synthetic organics.

3. Agricultural runoff yields synthetic organics such as pesticides and herbicides.

4. Water treatment operations can produce complex organics, such as trihalomethanes, during the disinfection process.

Most natural organic chemicals found in water are harmless, but some synthetic organic chemicals (SOCs) are considered to be carcinogenic or cause other adverse health effects at relatively low concentrations. In addition, some organic materials that are harmless in their natural state can react during disinfection processes to produce by-products with adverse health effects. Organic chemicals can also cause aesthetic problems such as tastes, odors, and color in water. TOC, a surrogate parameter, is currently regulated to estimate precursor levels, which may form disinfection by-products. Depending on the source water characteristics, a water system is required to remove a specified level of TOC.

Biological Characteristics

Biological characteristics correspond to the plants and animals, both dead and alive, that are found in water. They include viruses, bacteria, and other forms of aquatic life, as well as animal and plant contaminants.

Algae

Algae are an example of aquatic plants that can seriously affect the quality of surface water. Some algae cause taste-and-odor problems; others clog sand filters or produce slime growth on equipment, tanks, and reservoir walls. They are present to some extent in almost all surface water. Presence of algae in source waters can change other water characteristics, such as pH, and these changes can greatly impact the effectiveness of treatment processes within a plant. In addition, algae in source waters can also contribute to taste-and-odor episodes. For example, common earthy-musty tastes and odors in water are caused by geosmin and 2-methylisoborneol (MIB), which are produced by blue-green algae. Control of algae and other aquatic plants in lakes and reservoirs is discussed in *Water Treatment*, another book in this series.

Bacteria, viruses, and other microbiological constituents

Various types of bacteria can clog well screens, produce discolored water in the distribution system, or cause taste-and-odor problems. Of particular concern are bacteria and viruses that can cause disease in humans. These organisms do not ordinarily live in the water; they enter it through human or animal contact with the source water.

There are some disease-causing microscopic organisms that are not naturally found in water but can survive for a period of time after being deposited by humans or animals. Examples are protozoa (such as *Giardia lamblia* or *Cryptosporidium parvum*) that cause intestinal diseases in humans. A healthy person may not require any special medical attention, but immunocompromised people have died as a result of their exposure to these protozoa. Different disinfectants and other treatment technologies (e.g., membranes) are used to sanitize the water prior to its distribution for consumption.

Radioactive Constituents

Radionuclides can occur in water supplies either from natural sources or as a result of human activities. Naturally occurring radionuclides include radium 226, radium 228, and radon. None of these is usually present in significant amounts in surface waters but they do frequently occur in groundwater. Radon is a gas most often present in granite formations, where it flows through the fractures in the rock to an aquifer.

Radioactivity produced by human activities can also enter surface water supplies from a variety of sources. Fallout from nuclear weapons testing was at one time the most significant source of radioactivity in surface water, but the level gradually diminished after testing was stopped. Other potential sources include waste from medical, scientific, and industrial users of radionuclides; wastewater discharge from nuclear power plants; and discharges from the mining of radioactive materials.

FACTORS INFLUENCING SOURCE WATER QUALITY

Source water is affected primarily by the land around it or, in the case of groundwater, by the land over it. Land use practices can have a great effect on both surface water and groundwater, and the control of those practices is an important step in source water protection.

Surface Water Quality

Surface runoff

After rain strikes the earth and becomes surface runoff, the water begins to dissolve materials that it contacts and it takes on the characteristics of the land it passes over. Water flowing from remote areas of a watershed will not contain contaminants caused by human activities, but water passing over inhabited areas may contain many additional chemical and microbiological contaminants picked up in the flow across farmland and urban areas.

Agricultural runoff can contribute animal wastes, herbicides, pesticides, and fertilizer. Urban areas contribute a wide variety of organics and inorganics from homes, streets, pet wastes, stormwater overflows, sewage outfalls, and other sources.

Point and nonpoint sources

All waste contributions to a surface water source can be classified as either point or nonpoint sources. These terms are now widely used in environmental and pollution control regulations. They are important to the water supply operator because of their impact on water sources.

In simplest terms, a point source is a waste flow that comes out of a pipe. Under state and federal pollution control regulations, the quality of wastewater from point sources is regulated to prevent pollution of lakes and streams.

Wastes that flow over the ground into a lake or stream are termed nonpoint sources. These sources of water contamination are much harder to control because the source is often indefinite.

There are many ways in which water can become contaminated, and some of them may be due to sources hundreds of miles away. The factors that influence source water quality may be categorized as natural or human. Natural factors include

- climate,
- watershed characteristics,
- geology,
- microbial growth,
- fire,
- saltwater intrusion, and
- density (thermal stratification).

Human factors associated with point sources include

- wastewater discharges,
- industrial discharges,
- hazardous-waste facilities,
- mine drainage, and
- spills and releases.

Human factors associated with nonpoint sources include

- agricultural runoff,
- livestock,
- urban runoff,
- land development,
- landfills,
- erosion,
- atmospheric deposition, and
- recreational activities.

Water from reservoirs

Once runoff water enters a lake or storage reservoir, there can be other changes that take place—some beneficial and some not. As water enters a reservoir, suspended material in the flowing water begins to settle when the water becomes quiescent or slow-moving. While water is being held in a reservoir, bacterial action and natural oxidation can act on soluble contaminants and suspended particles to make them less likely to cause color, taste, and odor problems; sometimes the material will be converted into particles that will settle.

If a reservoir is large, it can absorb and dilute the shock loads of particularly turbid water received from streams following a storm. It may even be able to absorb and dilute a quantity of poor-quality water or a small chemical spill brought in by a stream. Wind action and algae usually keep the dissolved oxygen in a reservoir at beneficial levels, which helps natural purification processes and supports aquatic life.

Most bacteria that are pathogens, as well as protozoa that cause disease, are not natural to fresh water. Although some bacteria can survive for a fairly long time after leaving a human or animal, they cannot multiply. Eventually, most organisms will become nonviable and noninfectious when held in a reservoir for a period of time.

Algae are plants that contain chlorophyll. This means they can grow in water bodies exposed to light. There are three general categories of algae: diatoms, green algae, and blue-green algae.

Diatoms and green algae are found in reservoirs that have low nutrient levels and they help keep the water oxygenated. If they "bloom," or grow in profusion, they can clog intake screens and filters. At times, they can also cause taste-and-odor problems.

Blue-green algae are more commonly found in nutrient-rich waters where they can bloom profusely, especially when water temperatures are higher. Blue-green algae are notorious taste-and-odor producers and probably account for the bulk of such problems. Even though algae produce oxygen, the die-off of a sizable bloom can deplete the water of oxygen as bacterial decomposition of the dead algae proceeds.

All lakes progress through a natural process called eutrophication. In the early stages, plant life and fish are not produced. The lake then moves to a more advanced state of productivity and then to a point of overproductivity. Eventually, sediments fill the lake, and the lake becomes swampy or marshy. The eutrophication process usually takes centuries. All lakes are in one of the three stages, or somewhere in between.

The artificial introduction of nutrients into a lake from human activities can speed the eutrophication process. Lakes subjected to heavy loads of unnatural nutrients will have more frequent and serious algae blooms and may become unusable as water sources. Stopping the nutrient inflow or applying special treatment, such as aeration or chemical treatment, can sometimes restore such a lake to a useful state.

Additional details on treatment of lakes and reservoirs for algae and water weed control can be found in another book in this series, *Water Treatment*.

Atmospheric Contaminants

Airborne contamination is a nonpoint source that is very important and has received much attention in recent years. It is usually referred to as "acid rain."

The most common component of acid rain is sulfuric acid, which is generated in the atmosphere from the combustion by-products of coal used for power generation. It was believed for many years that building a high smokestack was the solution to the problem of coal combustion emissions. Local residents were not affected and the pollutants were carried "far away."

We now know that a process known as photochemical oxidation converts sulfur dioxide in the air to sulfuric acid. This acid can be carried hundreds of miles and then deposited as acid rain, acid snow, and even acid dust. Many lakes in the northeastern United States and Canada have had a definite change in the pH of their water in recent years due to acid rain. This has caused severe environmental damage to aquatic life and has solubilized metals such as aluminum. A secondary effect is the damage to forests, which serve to reduce erosion on watersheds.

Other sources of airborne contaminants are automobile exhaust, emissions from waste incinerators, volcanic eruptions, and almost any combustion process that does not include complete treatment of stack gases. The passage of strong clean-air legislation in 1990 and continued strengthening of clean-air standards in the future should help reduce the impact of atmospheric contamination.

Groundwater Quality

The quality of groundwater tends to be uniform throughout an aquifer. Changes in quality occur slowly. Groundwater is not as subject to direct pollution and contamination as surface water, except from leaky underground storage tanks or failure of onsite waste treatment systems.

Aquifer contamination

Because of the protective soil cover and the natural filtration provided by aquifer material, the biological characteristics of groundwater are generally very good. Because harmful bacteria do not penetrate very far into the soil, wells more than 50 ft (15 m) deep are generally free of harmful organisms. Some exceptions to this are aquifers fed by large voids in fractured rock or locations where there are holes (such as improperly abandoned wells) penetrating into the aquifer. Even if harmful bacteria do reach the aquifer, the hostile environment does not allow them to remain viable very long.

Most cases of groundwater contamination (Figure 6–7) are a result of either poor well construction or poor waste disposal practices on the land overlying the aquifer. Other sources of contamination may include recharge from nearby surface waters or excessive pumping near coastal areas, resulting in saltwater intrusion into the ambient groundwater. Movement of water in the ground can treat water naturally; many water supply systems, especially in European countries, employ riverbank-filtered water as their source of supply.

Chemical characteristics

Groundwater acquires its chemical characteristics in two ways: from the surface water that percolates into the aquifer and from the soil and rock that it contacts. Normal recharge for aquifers is the rain that falls on the aquifer recharge area. This water will generally be clean if the rain falls on land that is free from pollution; it generally won't be clean if the land is polluted. An example is agricultural land. Aquifer recharge from farmland water runoff can be contaminated with nitrates, herbicides, and pesticides.

Not all contamination of groundwater comes from surface contamination. A major problem in coastal areas is saltwater intrusion. Under natural conditions, the fresh water and salt water are in equilibrium. When the fresh water is removed from the aquifer faster than it is replenished, the salt water moves toward the wells. Under these conditions, wells may still be used, but the withdrawal must be limited to prevent further saltwater intrusion.

There are many other natural contaminants that affect the potability of groundwater. Some elements and compounds are beneficial or harmless in small amounts and become troublesome or harmful only when found in excessive quantities.

Other contaminants are harmful at very low levels, such as barium, arsenic, and various radionuclides. Gases that are undesirable in groundwater include hydrogen sulfide, methane, and radon. Common groundwater contaminants and their associated problems are listed in Table 6–4.

Chemical contaminants

The most serious contaminants found in public water supply wells are probably synthetic organic compounds. Over the years, chemicals have been carelessly disposed of on the ground, and they are now being found in many well supplies. Some of these chemicals are considered a health threat at concentrations far less than can be detected by taste or smell. The only way they can be detected is by relatively complicated and expensive tests. If chemical contamination of a well is detected, it is generally best to abandon the well and use another water source. If there is no alternative source, the chemicals can usually be removed from the water by aeration or carbon adsorption processes. It may be much more cost effective to avoid groundwater contamination than to treat the contaminated water. One common contaminant that makes groundwater unfit to drink is gasoline, which is a complex mixture of toxic organic compounds. Thousands of wells, mostly private individual home wells (but some public supplies, too), have been contaminated because of leaking underground gasoline tanks. Less widespread, but not uncommon, is contamination from underground fuel oil storage.

PUBLIC HEALTH SIGNIFICANCE OF WATER QUALITY

Water quality can have a significant effect on public health as a result of

- waterborne diseases,
- inorganic chemical contaminants,
- disinfectants and disinfection by-products (DBPs),
- organic chemical contaminants, and
- radioactive contaminants.

Waterborne Diseases

Continued source water protection efforts and improved treatment practices have resulted in an overall reduction of waterborne disease outbreaks over the years. Table 6–5 provides a summary of the reported waterborne disease outbreaks in the United States in recent years; however, it should be noted that most outbreaks are

TABLE 6–4 Common groundwater quality problems

Constituent	Source	Type of Problem	USEPA Primary Drinking Water Standards[*]	USEPA Secondary Drinking Water Standards[†]
		Inorganic Constituents		
Arsenic	Naturally occurring[‡]	Toxic	0.05 mg/L	—
Fluoride	Naturally occurring	Stains teeth, can cause tooth damage at high levels	4.0 mg/L	—
Hydrogen sulfide	Naturally occurring	Offensive odor, flammable, corrosive	—	0.05 mg/L
Iron	Naturally occurring	Stains plumbing fixtures and laundry, causes tastes	—	0.3 mg/L
Manganese	Naturally occurring	Discolors laundry and plumbing fixtures, causes tastes	—	0.05 mg/L
Nitrate	Fertilizer and fecal matter	Toxic to infants	10 mg/L (as nitrogen)	—
Radioactivity	Naturally occurring	Cancer causing	Gross alpha activity (15 pCi/L) Radium 226 and 228 (5 pCi/L)	—
Sodium	Naturally occurring	May contribute to high blood pressure	—	Being investigated
Sulfate	Naturally occurring[‡]	Laxative effect	—	250 mg/L
Total dissolved solids	Naturally occurring[‡]	Associated with tastes, scale formation, corrosion, and hardness	—	500 mg/L

Table continued next page

TABLE 6-4 Common groundwater quality problems *(continued)*

Constituent	Source	Type of Problem	USEPA Primary Drinking Water Standards*	USEPA Secondary Drinking Water Standards†
		Organic Constituents		
Pesticides and herbicides	Agricultural and industrial contamination	Many are toxic, cause tastes and odors	Several are regulated	—
Solvents	Industrial contamination	Many are toxic, cause tastes and odors	Being developed	—
		Microbiological Constituents		
Disease-causing microorganisms	Fecal contamination	Cause variety of illnesses	Coliform bacteria are regulated as indicator organism	—
Iron bacteria	Contamination from surface	Produce foul-smelling slimes, which plug well screens, pumps, and valves	—	—
Sulfate-reducing bacteria	Contamination from surface	Produce foul-smelling and corrosive hydrogen sulfide	—	—

Source: Basics of Well Construction Operator's Guide.

* State regulations may be more restrictive.
† Not enforceable at federal level.
‡ The naturally occurring elements can also be present as a result of contamination by humans.

Source: Monitoring and Assessing Water Quality, National Water Quality Inventory: 1998 Report to Congress, Chapter 7, page 6, USEPA.

FIGURE 6–7 Sources of groundwater contamination

TABLE 6–5 Waterborne disease outbreaks in the United States, 1980 to 1996[*][†]

Illness	Number of Outbreaks	Cases of Illness
Gastroenteritis, undefined	183	55,562
Giardiasis	84	10,262
Chemical poisoning	46	3,097
Shigellosis	19	3,864
Gastroenteritis, Norwalk virus	15	9,437
Campylobacteriosis	15	2,480
Hepatitis A	13	412
Cryptosporidiosis	10	419,939[‡]
Salmonellosis	5	1,845
Gastroenteritis, *Escherichia coli* 0157:H7	3	278
Yersiniosis	2	103
Cholera	2	28
Gastroenteritis, rotavirus	1	1,761
Typhoid fever	1	60
Gastroenteritis, *Plesiomonas*	1	60
Amoebiasis	1	4
Cyclosporiasis	1	21
Total	**402**	**509,213**

Source: Water Quality and Treatment, 5th ed., *1999, AWWA, Chapter 2, Table 2.1, p. 2.4.*

[*]An outbreak of waterborne disease for microorganisms is defined as (1) two or more persons experience a similar illness after consumption or use of water intended for drinking, and (2) epidemiologic evidence implicates the water as a source of illness. A single case of chemical poisoning constitutes an outbreak in a laboratory study indicates that the water has been contaminated by the chemical.

[†]Data are from the Centers for Disease Control and Prevention annual surveillance summaries for 1980 through 1985 and 2-year summaries for 1986 through 1994, as corrected for several missing outbreaks by G.F. Craun (personal communications).

[‡]Total includes 403,000 cases from a single outbreak.

generally not reported. Outbreaks are usually caused by the use of contaminated source water, ineffective treatment operations, or contamination in the water distribution system. Even though modern treatment will remove or inactivate known disease-causing organisms to safe levels, it is still desirable to have an uncontaminated source of water. Waterborne diseases are generally acute and of short duration, and symptoms are similar to those of diseases caused by other factors, such as contaminated or uncooked food. Table 6–6 lists the causes and health effects of common waterborne diseases. The sources of disease-causing organisms in water include wastewater treatment plant discharges, surface runoff containing human or animal fecal contamination, or contribution from an onsite waste treatment system (e.g., septic tanks). The single most prevalent waterborne

TABLE 6–6 Potential waterborne disease-causing organisms

Organism	Major Disease	Primary Source
Bacteria		
Salmonella typhi	Typhoid fever	Human feces
Salmonella paratyphi	Paratyphoid fever	Human feces
Other *Salmonella* sp.	Gastroenteritis (salmonellosis)	Human/animal feces
Shigella	Bacillary dysentery	Human feces
Vibrio cholerae	Cholera	Human feces, coastal water
Pathogenic *Escherichia coli*	Gastroenteritis	Human/animal feces
Yersinia enterocolitica	Gastroenteritis	Human/animal feces
Campylobacter jejuni	Gastroenteritis	Human/animal feces
Legionella pneumophila	Legionnaires' disease, Pontiac fever	Warm water
Mycobacterium avium intracellulare	Pulmonary disease	Human/animal feces, soil, water
Pseudomonas aeruginosa	Dermatitis	Natural waters
Aeromonas hydrophila	Gastroenteritis	Natural waters
Helicobacter pylori	Peptic ulcers	Saliva, human feces?

Table continued next page

TABLE 6–6 Potential waterborne disease-causing organisms *(continued)*

Organism	Major Disease	Primary Source
	Enteric Viruses	
Poliovirus	Poliomyelitis	Human feces
Coxsackievirus	Upper respiratory disease	Human feces
Echovirus	Upper respiratory disease	Human feces
Rotavirus	Gastroenteritis	Human feces
Norwalk virus and other caliciviruses	Gastroenteritis	Human feces
Hepatitis A virus	Infectious hepatitis	Human feces
Hepatitis E virus	Hepatitis	Human feces
Astrovirus	Gastroenteritis	Human feces
Enteric adenoviruses	Gastroenteritis	Human feces
	Protozoa and other organisms	
Giardia lamblia	Giardiasis (gastroenteritis)	Human and animal feces
Cryptosporidium parvum	Cryptosporidiosis (gastroenteritis)	Human and animal feces
Entamoeba histolytica	Amoebic dysentery	Human feces
Cyclospora cayatanensis	Gastroenteritis	Human feces
Microspora	Gastroenteritis	Human feces
Acanthamoeba	Eye infection	Soil and water
Toxoplasma gondii	Flu-like symptoms	Cats
Naegleria fowleri	Primary amoebic meningoencephalitis	Soil and water
Blue-green algae	Gastroenteritis, liver damage, nervous system damage	Natural waters
Fungi	Respiratory allergies	Air, water?

Source: Water Quality and Treatment, 5th ed., *1999, AWWA, Chapter 2, Table 2.2, p. 2.5.*

disease is giardiasis. *G. lamblia*, the cause of the disease, is a protozoan that can infect both humans and animals. Two common carriers are beavers and muskrats, which, by their very nature, are commonly found around surface water bodies. The organism has a cyst form that can remain viable under adverse conditions in water for 1 to 3 months. The cysts are quite resistant to chlorine and can pass through filters that are not operating efficiently. Cryptosporidiosis, caused by another protozoan known as *Cryptosporidium*, is associated with most reported cases of illness due to waterborne outbreaks.

Cryptosporidium parvum oocysts, the species that causes disease in humans, is smaller in size than the *Giardia* cyst and is also more resistant to chlorine disinfection. However, well-operated filtration plants along with use of other disinfectants (e.g., ozone, chlorine dioxide, and UV light) are effective control measures.

Most reported outbreaks that are traceable to a water supply originate from unfiltered water systems or contaminated water sources (surface as well as groundwater), but there have also been outbreaks that resulted when filtered water systems were not functioning properly.

Waterborne disease organisms are extremely difficult to detect directly. In spite of many advances in laboratory technology, only very large, well-equipped laboratories can perform the tests for specific organisms. The presence of microbial contamination is detected by analyzing for surrogate microbial parameters, such as total coliforms, heterotrophic plate counts, or *Escherichia coli*. Positive detection of these parameters may indicate possible contamination and further evaluation. Confirmed contamination may require public notification and identification and rectification of the causes of contamination.

Inorganic Chemical Contaminants

Inorganic contaminants are primarily the metals found in water, but other compounds and materials are included. Some inorganic contaminants (e.g., arsenic) are associated with source water, and others (e.g., lead and asbestos) can be added to water during distribution. Some inorganic contaminants are suspected carcinogens (e.g., lead and arsenic). Regulatory standards have been established for the allowable concentrations of most inorganic contaminants, though others are still being considered for regulation. Some are highly toxic, and some are only mildly toxic. The list includes

Aluminum	Ammonia	Antimony
Arsenic	Asbestos	Barium
Beryllium	Boron	Cadmium
Chromium	Copper	Cyanide
Fluoride	Lead	Manganese

Mercury	Molybdenum	Nickel
Nitrate	Nitrite	Selenium
Silver	Sodium	Strontium
Sulfate	Thallium	Vanadium
Zinc		

Disinfectants

Chlorine is an inorganic chemical contaminant but it is generally listed along with other disinfectants. Although chlorine is now being considered as either a direct or indirect cause of some adverse health effects, it should be remembered that its use has saved thousands (if not millions) of lives since it was introduced as a water disinfectant. State and federal regulations are steadily moving toward requiring mandatory chlorination of all public water supplies.

Other disinfectants in common use are chlorine dioxide, ozone, and potassium permanganate. It is likely that UV disinfection will be commonly used in the future because it can effectively inactivate both *G. lamblia* and *C. parvum*. These chemicals have some advantages for use in drinking water disinfection but their principal disadvantage is that they do not provide a disinfectant residual that will remain in the water for a period of time. Therefore, chlorine in the free or combined form will be the chemical of choice for maintaining disinfectant residual in the distribution system. As part of the Stage 1 Disinfectant/Disinfection By-Products Rule that became effective in January 2002 for systems serving more than 10,000 persons, disinfectant residuals will be controlled in the finished water to minimize their associated health effects.

Other methods of disinfecting water include the use of iodine, bromine, silver, and hydrogen peroxide. However, these methods are rarely used to disinfect public drinking water supplies.

Chlorine

All forms of chlorination, including gaseous chlorine, liquid chlorine, sodium hypochlorite, and calcium hypochlorite, produce hypochlorous acid in dilute water solution. For killing or inactivating pathogens, hypochlorous acid is the most effective of the various chlorine compounds that occur when water is chlorinated. All chlorine disinfectants are strong chemicals and are very toxic to plants and animals in high concentrations. At the low concentrations used for water disinfection, they are considered to have very low toxicity.

Free chlorine reacts with some of the natural organic compounds present in raw water to form varying amounts of chemicals that fall into a group called trihalomethanes (THMs). The principal THM is chloroform. These compounds, as a group, are considered carcinogenic. Consequently, state and federal regulations limit the amount of THMs that may be present in water provided to the public. It has also been found that chlorine and other disinfectants react with contaminants in water to create many additional compounds, some of which are likely to cause adverse health effects. These substances have been grouped under the general heading of DBPs. DBPs are still under study, but it appears certain that additional regulations will be imposed on disinfection practices in future years to minimize exposure of the public to certain DBPs.

Chloramine

Chloramine is a disinfectant that is formed when chlorine reacts with ammonia in the water. Chloramine reduces tastes and odors in some water and produces a lower concentration of THMs but it does not have the disinfecting power of free chlorine against bacteria. It is also considered relatively ineffective for inactivating *Giardia*.

Ozone

Ozone is a form of oxygen and a very powerful oxidant and disinfectant. It is widely used in Europe and is rapidly becoming popular in the United States. It destroys organic matter and is very effective against bacteria, viruses, *Giardia*, and *Cryptosporidium*. It quickly disappears in water, however, and consequently does not have a protective residual effect in the distribution system. When ozone is used as an initial disinfectant for water, it must be followed by the addition of chlorine to provide a disinfectant residual. Ozone is produced by an electrical discharge in the presence of an oxygen-rich atmosphere and must be produced on site. Both the initial capital costs for equipment and the operating costs of using ozone are quite high in comparison with those for chlorine.

Organic Chemical Contaminants

Organic contaminants in drinking water come from the following three major sources:

1. the breakdown of naturally occurring organic materials;
2. contamination from industrial, commercial, and domestic activities; and
3. reactions that take place during water treatment and distribution.

The first source is by far the largest. It consists of breakdown products from the decay of leaves and other plant material, aquatic animal death and decomposition, algae decomposition, and other natural aquatic life by-products. Most of these organics, except for some high molecular aliphatic and aromatic hydrocarbons, have no direct adverse health effects. Upon disinfection of water, some of these organics produce DBPs, which do have potential adverse health effects. The chemicals that enter water from industrial, commercial, and domestic activities include those used in agriculture, found in sewage discharges, and washed from contaminated land or urban runoff. This group, by far, contains the greatest number of chemicals of concern—solvents, pesticides, herbicides, and other organics used by the business community and the public. There are regulations covering the use and disposal of many of these chemicals, and more and more chemicals will be controlled in the future. Many of these organic compounds are regulated in drinking water. One of the best-known groups of organic chemicals is the polychlorinated biphenyls (PCBs). Discharge of PCBs in industrial wastes has generated immense publicity and controversy. Laboratory tests indicate that very low concentrations of PCBs fed to animals can cause cancer. Another highly publicized chemical is dioxin, which appears to be a potent animal carcinogen. The principles, occurrence, and control of organic chemicals in drinking water are covered in detail in *Water Quality*, part of this series.

A number of these organic compounds, referred to as endocrine disruptors, potentially affect the development and reproduction functions in humans and other animals by interfering with the production of hormones. These compounds, if not already regulated, are also targeted for future regulation.

Radioactive Contaminants

Radioactivity is a frightening subject for the general public. The terror of nuclear war has colored every mention of radioactivity or nuclear waste. It must be emphasized that the radioactivity found in water is almost always from natural sources. Therefore, groundwater sources have the potential of containing radionuclides. All radioactive contaminants are carcinogenic. The radionuclides of concern in drinking water are

- uranium;
- gross alpha and beta emitters;
- radium 226;
- radium 228;
- radioactive cesium, iodine, and strontium 89 and 90;
- radon;
- thorium 230; and
- thorium 232.

The unit commonly used to express radiation dosage is the "rem." Generally, radiation expressed in equivalent rems from different radionuclides produces the same biological effects. Humans are subjected to some radiation from cosmic rays from space, radiation from the soil and rocks in the environment, and X rays. The average annual dose from all sources is about 200 millirems (mrem) per year. The US Environmental Protection Agency (USEPA) estimates that radioactivity in drinking water contributes about 0.1 to 3 percent of the annual dose received by an average person. This can vary greatly, however, and the radionuclide that is usually responsible is radon. It is estimated that between 500 and 4,000 public water supplies have radon at levels that create an equivalent dose of 100 mrem per year.

It is currently estimated that up to 30,000 water systems have radon at a level at which some human risk can be calculated. However, the greatest public exposure to radon comes from soils that underlie house basements. Radon gas is released from the soil and can enter the living space through cracks if the basement is not sealed. The relative impact of waterborne radon and soil-released radon on public health is still a matter of some controversy.

PUBLIC WATER SUPPLY REGULATIONS

Generally, federal, state, or local agencies regulate drinking water. Regulations for operating and monitoring water systems serving the public were developed by each state during the early 1900s, but the policies and degree of enforcement varied considerably among the states. Prior to 1974, federal involvement in regulating the provision of drinking water to the public consisted only of the development of drinking water standards by the US Public Health Service. These standards suggested bacterial and chemical limits for water from public water systems. The first drinking water standard was passed in 1914 to control *E. coli* in water supplies used by interstate carriers. In 1925, additional standards were developed for physical and chemical constituents in drinking water. By 1962, 28 contaminants were regulated, but these standards regulated less than 2 percent of US water supply systems. Although the standards were not federally enforceable, they were incorporated into the regulations of most states. Each state's health department generally monitored water quality, enforced regulations, and provided technical assistance to water system operators.

The Safe Drinking Water Act

During the 1960s and early 1970s, scientists and public health experts discovered a previously unrecognized potential for harmful disease-causing organisms and chemicals in drinking water. There was also increasing pressure by the public and legislators to create uniform national standards for drinking water to ensure that every public water supply in the country met minimum health standards.

In response to these concerns, Congress passed the Safe Drinking Water Act (SDWA) in 1974. The SDWA directs the USEPA to establish standards and requirements necessary to protect the public from all known harmful contaminants in drinking water. It also asks each state to accept primary enforcement responsibility (primacy) for enforcing the federal requirements. Since its inception, the SDWA has been amended, or reauthorized, several times, with the most notable amendments in 1986 and 1996. The original SDWA and the 1986 amendments focussed on treatment in order to provide safe drinking water. The 1996 amendments included source water protection, operator training, and funding for water system improvements as important aspects of safe drinking water.

SDWA provisions

Many requirements in the SDWA relate to public water system operation, monitoring, and reporting. The more important points of the regulations are as follows:

- Based on available sound science and cost-effective technologies, the USEPA establishes primary drinking water standards for microbiological and chemical contaminants that may be found in drinking water and that could cause adverse health effects for humans. The maximum concentration that is allowable is called the maximum contaminant level (MCL). All states must make their regulations at least as stringent as the MCLs established by the USEPA. The primary standards are mandatory, and all public water systems in the United States must comply with them.

- The USEPA establishes secondary drinking water standards that set recommended MCLs for contaminants that are not a direct threat to public health but affect aesthetic qualities such as tastes, odors, color, and staining of fixtures. The secondary standards are strongly recommended but not enforceable.

- SDWA mandates states to have certification programs and recertification requirements for water system operators and to ensure that small water systems have the technical, financial, and managerial capacity to provide safe drinking water.

- Public notification (PN) is required by the SDWA as the first step of enforcement against all public water systems that fail to comply with federal requirements. Systems that violate operating, monitoring, or reporting requirements or that exceed an MCL must inform the public of the problem and explain the public health significance of their violation. In addition, SDWA requires all community water systems to prepare and distribute annual consumer confidence reports, including sources of water and detected contaminants and their associated health effects.

- SDWA mandates states to conduct an assessment of its sources of drinking water to identify potential sources of contamination.
- Federal enforcement, including stiff monetary fines, may be leveled against water systems that do not comply with the federal requirements.
- A public water system is defined as a system that supplies piped water for human consumption and has at least 15 service connections or 25 or more persons who are served by the system for 60 or more days a year.

Provisions of the SDWA and regulations enacted by the USEPA are explained in detail in *Water Quality*, which is also part of this series.

Classes of public water systems

In implementing the requirements of the SDWA, the USEPA divided public water systems into three categories based on the number and type of customers served:

1. *Community public water systems* are those water utilities that serve the same customers year-round. Examples are municipal systems, rural water districts, and mobile home parks.

2. *Nontransient, noncommunity public water systems* are entities that have their own water supply that serves the same customers for more than 6 months but not year-round. Examples include schools, factories, and office buildings.

3. *Transient, noncommunity public water systems* have their own water system that serves customers but not the same individuals for more than 6 months a year. Examples include parks, motels, campgrounds, restaurants, and churches.

Community and nontransient, noncommunity water systems are required to meet specific operating requirements and to perform relatively extensive monitoring of water quality. This is necessary because their customers use the water over a long period of time and could experience adverse health effects from continuous exposure to relatively low levels of contaminants. The requirements for transient, noncommunity systems are not as stringent because the customers use the water only occasionally.

Water systems having fewer than 25 customers and individual homes having their own source of water (such as a well) are referred to as private or nonpublic water systems. Nonpublic systems are not covered by the SDWA but are usually regulated by state and/or local jurisdictions.

State Drinking Water Programs

The intent of the SDWA is for each state to accept primary enforcement responsibility for operation of the drinking water program within their state. To be given primacy, a state must implement all requirements, standards, and programs required by the USEPA. In return, the state receives a federal grant to supplement state funds to operate the public water supply program.

Most states also have programs in addition to those mandated by the USEPA. These include certification of water system operators, cross-connection control, and monitoring for contaminants that are not part of the federal requirements.

The major functions provided by state drinking water primacy agencies are as follows:

- *Monitoring and tracking*. The state staff must ensure that all systems perform the proper monitoring, use approved laboratories, and regularly submit reports on system operation.

- *Sanitary surveys*. A sanitary survey is an onsite inspection of a water system's facilities and operation. Surveys are performed by state staff or other qualified persons on a regular basis. Reports are prepared for the system owner or operator and problems or deficiencies are identified.

- *Plan review*. The SDWA requires that states review and approve all plans for water system construction and major improvements.

- *Technical assistance*. One function of the state program is to provide water system owners and operators with technical assistance when they have problems.

- *Laboratory services*. Chemical, radiological, and microbiological analyses of water quality must be performed by a certified laboratory. In some states, state laboratories perform all or most of the tests. Other states certify commercial laboratories that do the work for the water systems.

- *Enforcement*. The SDWA requires states to use enforcement actions when federal requirements are violated.

As the federal requirements are periodically changed and expanded, each state must, within a prescribed period of time, make similar changes in its regulations and begin implementation and enforcement.

SELECTED SUPPLEMENTARY READINGS

Basics of Well Construction Operator's Guide. 1986. Denver, Colo.: American Water Works Association.

Manual M7, Problem Organisms in Water: Identification and Treatment. 1995. Denver, Colo.: American Water Works Association.

Manual of Instruction for Water Treatment Plant Operators. 1975. Albany, N.Y.: New York State Department of Health.

Manual of Water Utility Operations, 8th ed. 1988. Austin, Tex.: Texas Water Utilities Association.

Monitoring and Assessing Water Quality, National Water Quality Inventory: 1998 Report to Congress. USEPA. Available: http://www.epa.gov/305b/98Report/Chap7.pdf.

Safe Drinking Water Advisor: A Compliance Assistance Resource. Denver, Colo.: American Water Works Association (subscription service).

VOCs and Unregulated Contaminants. 1990. Denver, Colo.: American Water Works Association.

Water Quality and Treatment, 5th ed. 1999. New York: McGraw-Hill and American Water Works Association (available from AWWA).

Water Source Protection

The quality of source water is subject to threats both from nature and from human activities. Natural threats include saltwater intrusion, errant microbiological growth, and fire. In general, natural factors cannot be controlled. Human threats can be categorized as point or nonpoint sources. Point sources include wastewater treatment plant discharges, hazardous-waste facilities, mine drainage, and spills and releases. Nonpoint sources include agricultural and urban runoff, landfills, erosion, and recreational activities (such as boating on reservoirs). It is the operator's responsibility to minimize harm from both natural and human threats. Surface water sources are more directly contaminated by human causes, but as has been found in recent years, groundwater sources can also be affected.

A great amount of information can be gained by contacting the US Environmental Protection Agency (USEPA) or a state-level government organization charged with protecting drinking water supplies. The USEPA Web site contains valuable information regarding protection of both raw ground and surface water sources: http://www.epa.gov/safewater/protect.html.

FUNDAMENTAL PRINCIPLES

Surface water can usually recover from pollution incidents much faster than groundwater. However, it is also more susceptible to the assaults of nature, such as flooding, droughts, or algae blooms.

Impacts to a groundwater source are less frequent, but when they do occur, natural recovery is generally very slow. Some threats to a water source are relatively obvious, as in the installation of a gasoline storage tank next to a well or shoreline grazing of a herd of cattle along a small reservoir. Unfortunately, most threats are not this obvious, and many are difficult to identify, even with time and hard work.

Source Protection Area

The first step in source protection is to identify the area that needs protection and who has an interest in protecting it. All of the water system's customers should be interested and kept informed of potential threats to water quantity or quality. Farmers and business people who might be in the protection area have a financial stake in preventing pollution, so they should be involved. Municipal and county officials may have to act as an enforcement arm, so they should be involved, and public health and environmental protection agencies should also be kept informed. When all interested parties have been contacted and, optimally, when a task force has been formed, the job can begin.

Aquifer delineation

Groundwater comes from an aquifer that is recharged by percolating and infiltrating surface water. The only way to tell what surface water is recharging a well's aquifer is to define the land area over the portion of the aquifer used by the well. This land area is called the aquifer recharge area or the wellhead protection area (WHPA).

In the past, many states used a fixed radius around a well to determine the protected area. This was commonly 100 ft (30 m) for a private well and as little as 300 ft (90 m) for a public water supply well. Utilities were sometimes required to own the land within that circle or to at least have control over its use.

If a well is relatively deep and properly constructed, protection of a fixed radius around the well is probably adequate in most cases for protection from microbiological contaminants. However, this fixed radius has been found to have little bearing on contamination from chemicals. Some chemicals have been found to travel up to thousands of feet within an aquifer. In other words, depending on local geological formations, a relatively small area or a very large area may be required from the WHPA.

If the region is one that has already had its groundwater mapped by the US Geological Survey (USGS) or a state geology department, information on the recharge area for a well may be readily available. Unless the area is one with very easily determined borders, it is best for a utility to hire a firm having experts in geology, hydrology, and mapping of aquifers for further characterization.

Watershed mapping

If a water utility uses a surface water source, the watershed boundary (or drainage area) should be determined. The outside boundary of a watershed is the surface water divide between watersheds. All water falling as rain or snow flows toward gradually larger waterways. As illustrated in Figure 7–1, various types of maps can be used in watershed mapping and for identifying surface features. The most accurately drawn watersheds use topographical maps like the one shown in Figure 7–2.

Source: Protecting Local Ground-Water Supplies Through Wellhead Protection *(1991).*

FIGURE 7–1 Various types of maps that can be used in watershed mapping

★ Third Street Dam

Source: Pennsylvania Spatial Data Access Web site: www.pasda/psu.edu/access/quad.

FIGURE 7-2 A typical topographical map of a watershed

USGS topographic maps are particularly useful for outlining a watershed. The ridges between watersheds are easily identified. Water on one side of a ridge flows toward one watershed, and water on the other side flows in another direction. Using lines to connect the ridges on the map will outline the area contributing water to the source used by a water system.

Once a watershed has been identified, the topographic maps can also be used to identify the general types of vegetation and activities that exist within the drainage area. Features such as forests, open land, roads, industrial activities, and houses that were present when the map was prepared are all shown. These data can be useful in determining the stream flow characteristics in addition to potential sources of contamination in the watershed.

Sources of Contamination

When the WHPA or watershed boundary for a water source has been determined, the next step is to develop a complete inventory of the potential contamination sources within the area. This does not have to be an expensive project, and it does not have to be done by water utility personnel. It could become a public service project; local volunteers from scouting, senior citizens, service clubs, and volunteer fire department groups have proven very effective in doing the job.

Each volunteer or group is furnished with a map, or a portion of a map, and asked to mark potential contamination sources on it. A list of common sources (Table 7–1) should be furnished to the volunteers. Detailed information on locations of particular concern can be compiled by the volunteers or followed up by more experienced personnel.

Local and area zoning maps and master plans should also be reviewed to identify possible future sources of contamination from industrial parks, pipelines, sewage treatment plants, waste disposal sites, and similar threatening developments. In addition, state environmental agencies can be contacted regarding their records of underground storage tanks (USTs) or other permitted discharges to surface waters.

Once all the data have been collected, the threats to source water quality can be ranked. Table 7–2 is an excerpt from a susceptibility analysis conducted during a source water assessment for a reservoir in Pennsylvania. Figure 7–3 contains an overview and matrix definitions for this assessment.

A potential source of concern for both groundwater and surface water sources is how the contamination of one affects the quality of the other. Little effort has been made to measure the extent of impact, but it is commonly known that contaminated surface water entering the phreatic zone (the saturated, subsurface zone) will mix with and contaminate cleaner groundwater supplies. In addition, contaminated groundwater discharging to wetlands and streams can impact their quality. Although the interaction varies from simple to complex, it is important to consider groundwater and surface water as one hydrologic system.

Vandalism and Terrorism

September 11, 2001, was a day that changed all security system operations for the foreseeable future. Rumors and threats of biological terrorism aimed at water systems were commonplace in the year following New York's World Trade Center attacks. Concern over high-hazard dams, water treatment facilities, and inlet and outlet pipes precipitated the development of vulnerability assessment methodologies.

TABLE 7–1 Common sources of groundwater contamination

Category	Contaminant Source	
Agricultural	Animal burial areas	Irrigation sites
	Animal feedlots	Manure-spreading areas or pits
	Fertilizer storage or use	Pesticide storage or use
Commercial	Airports	Jewelry or metal plating
	Auto repair shops	Laundromats
	Boat yards	Medical institutions
	Construction areas	Paint shops
	Car washes	Photography establishments
	Cemeteries	Railroad tracks and yards
	Dry cleaners	Research laboratories
	Gas stations	Scrap and junkyards
	Golf courses	Storage tanks
Industrial	Asphalt plants	Petroleum production or storage
	Chemical manufacture or storage	Pipelines
	Electronics manufacture	Septic lagoons and sludge
	Electroplaters	Storage tanks
	Foundries or metal fabricators	Toxic and hazardous spills
	Machine or metalworking shops	Wells (operating or abandoned)
	Mining and mine drainage	Wood-preserving facilities
Residential	Fuel oil	Septic systems or cesspools
	Furniture stripping or refinishing	Sewer lines
	Household hazardous products	Swimming pools (chemicals)
	Household lawns	
Other	Hazardous-waste landfills	Recycling or reduction facilities
	Municipal incinerators	Road-deicing operations
	Municipal landfills	Road maintenance depots
	Municipal sewer lines	Stormwater drains or basins
	Open burning sites	Transfer stations

Although water utility personnel can be thankful that no major violence or violent acts have been associated with water sources or water supply to any important extent, it has been incumbent upon them to make security a priority. Even in countries at war or suffering from civil unrest, water supplies have not yet been used as agents to carry toxic or disease-causing materials. However, the possibility of vandalism or terrorism aimed at a water system must be seriously considered, and it should be part of any utility emergency plan.

TABLE 7-2 Susceptibility analysis for the Crum Creek Watershed

Activity	Matrix A Potential for Contamination	Matrix B	Matrix C Potential Impact	Matrix D Susceptibility Rating
Spills in Zone A	**High** Short travel time, high persistence	**High** High quantity, high A result	**High** High sensitivity, high B result	**A** No control practices, high C result
Spills in Zone B	**High** Medium travel time, high persistence	**High** High quantity, high A result	**High** High sensitivity, high B result	**A** No control practices, high C result
1. 33-in. Sewage pipe	**High** Short travel time, medium persistence	**High** Medium quantity, high A result	**High** High sensitivity, high B result	**D** Regulated containment, high C result
2. Waterfowl	**Medium** Short travel time, low persistence	**Low** Low quantity—domestic level, medium A result	**Medium** High sensitivity, low B result	**B** No control practices, medium C result
3. Development	**Medium** Short travel time, low persistence	**Low** Low quantity—domestic level, medium A result	**Medium** High sensitivity, low B result	**D** Non-point source with best management practices, medium C result
4. Sewage lift station	**Medium** Short travel time, low persistence	**Medium** Medium quantity, medium A result	**High** High sensitivity, medium B result	**D** Regulated containment, high C result
5. Sewage lift station	**Medium** Short travel time, low persistence	**Medium** Medium quantity, medium A result	**High** High sensitivity, medium B result	**D** Regulated containment, high C result

POTENTIAL FOR CONTAMINATION
MATRIX A — Time of Travel vs. Persistence

Time of Travel	Short	Medium	Long
Surface Water Intakes	Zone A = 5 hours	Zone B = 25 hours	Zone C = remainder of watershed

Persistence	High	Medium	Low
Contaminant ability to move in the environment	If contaminant has been known to contaminate water with concentration greater than the MCL or in significant concentration.	Significant concentrations contaminate water, but may be partially removed by geologic materials.	If area's geology allows for removal of the contaminant

MATRIX B — Matrix A vs. Quantity

Quantity	High	Medium	Low
	Clearly associated with commercial- or industrial-sized operations with a minimum 10x a reportable release, event, or equivalent	Reportable releases, events, up to 10x those quantities associated with commercial- or industrial-sized operations	Clearly on a domestic level

POTENTIAL IMPACT
MATRIX C — Potential for Contamination (Result of Matrix B) vs. Sensitivity

Sensitivity	High	Medium	Low
Sensitivity of drinking water to contaminants	Surface water sources—short travel times, limited processes for mitigation (Zone A)	Longer travel times, some ability to mitigate (Zone B)	Overlying geologic materials are expected to provide some treatment for infiltrating water (Zone C)

SUSCEPTIBILITY RATING
MATRIX D — Potential for Release (from Potential for Release Table) vs. Potential Impact (Result of Matrix C)

Methodology taken from the Commonwealth of Pennsylvania's Source Water Assessment and Protection Program document (document 383-5000-001 at the following Web site: http://www.dep.state.pa.us/dep/subject/All_Final_Technical_guidance/bwsch/bwsch.htm)

FIGURE 7–3 Susceptibility analysis of drinking water sources to contamination definitions of matrix terms (Pennsylvania Dept. of Environmental Protection, 2000)

If water were delivered to customers in small volumes to be used exclusively for drinking, it would be relatively easy for a terrorist to add enough dangerous material to cause human illness. However, the fact that drinking and cooking account for only a small portion of the water delivered to customers by a public water system is an important safety factor. It means that a rather large volume of poison would have to be introduced to the water supply to create a high enough concentration to cause sickness from drinking the water.

During World War II, many utilities took serious measures to safeguard water sources as well as treatment and pumping facilities. The threat to these facilities is a much more believable scenario. Arson or use of explosives could easily prevent the delivery of water to at least a portion of the transmission and distribution system for most water utilities. Prevention of those acts is practical only in the face of a threat, but responding to the results of such acts should be considered a part of every utility's emergency plans. Fires and explosions are much more likely to happen as a result of human error or an accident than of malice.

The events of Sept. 11, 2001, have made the world more cognizant of potential weaknesses in every infrastructure, including our water systems. In response to these concerns, the USEPA and the US Department of Energy (Sandia Laboratories) have taken many actions to improve the security of the nation's drinking water, wastewater infrastructure, transmission lines, and dams, including the following:

- *Alerts and notices*—sent to all utilities and local law enforcement outlining security measures, resources available, and advice on monitoring and treatment.

- *Vulnerability assessments and remediation plans*—tools for drinking water utilities have been developed and are being tested.

- *Model emergency operations plans*—being developed for both waste and drinking water systems.

- *General security overview*—training developed through partnership with American Water Works Association covers an entire spectrum of security issues.

- *Vulnerability assessment overview and implementation*—detailed presentations and workshops on what constitutes an effective vulnerability assessment for drinking water utilities and how they can be applied.

- *Information sharing*—the development of a secure Information Sharing and Analysis Center, which partners the Association of Metropolitan Water Agencies, the FBI, and the USEPA.

GROUNDWATER PROTECTION

Groundwater protection can be instituted at federal, state, and local levels. There are an increasing number of groundwater protection programs and regulations, especially in areas where there are real threats to groundwater quality and/or quantity. These regulations generally require permits for well installation and have had increasing impact on land use planning.

Federal-level Aquifer Protection

Because a large number of people depend on it for their water needs, groundwater is an important resource that must be protected. Even though many serious groundwater contamination incidents have occurred, and new ones will continue to happen, the public and regulators are becoming more aware that protection is necessary. Figure 7–4 illustrates some of the many potential sources of groundwater contamination.

One example of an interstate authority with a major focus on groundwater quantity/quality is the Delaware River Basin Commission (DRBC). The DRBC has implemented groundwater protected area regulations within its region of concern, including portions of the states of Pennsylvania, New York, and Delaware. See the DRBC Web site for more information (http://www.state.nj.us/drbc).

Sole-source aquifers

One mechanism for protecting an aquifer is to have it designated as a sole-source aquifer. Under provisions of the Safe Drinking Water Act (SDWA), the USEPA can, on its own initiative or as the result of a petition, designate an aquifer as a sole source for an area. After a determination is published, no federal money may be used or granted for any purpose that could result in the contamination of that aquifer.

By 2002, 71 aquifers had been designated as "sole-source" within the United States. Sole-source protection has been granted to aquifers as small as those located on rocky islands off the coast of Maine and as large as the 175-mi-long (282-km-long) Edwards Aquifer that supplies the San Antonio, Texas, area. The Edwards Aquifer was the first to receive sole-source designation under the SDWA. A map showing locations of sole-source aquifers can be obtained from USEPA's Office of Ground Water and Drinking Water, or at its Web site (http://www.epa.gov/safewater/swp/sumssa.html).

Source: Wellhead Protection *(1987).*

FIGURE 7-4 Sources of groundwater contamination

Other environmental regulations

There are a number of other national laws that protect aquifers, including:

- The Resource Conservation and Recovery Act (RCRA), which regulates the storage, transportation, treatment, and disposal of solid and hazardous wastes. It is principally designed to prevent contaminants from leaching into groundwater from municipal landfills, underground storage tanks, surface impoundments, and hazardous-waste disposal facilities.

- The Comprehensive Environmental Response, Compensation, and Liability Act (Superfund), which authorizes the government to clean up contamination caused by chemical spills or hazardous-waste sites that could (or already do) pose threats to the environment. It also allows citizens to sue violators of the law and establishes "community right-to-know" programs.

- The Federal Insecticide, Fungicide, and Rodenticide Act (FIFRA), which authorizes the USEPA to control the availability of pesticides that have the ability to leach into groundwater.

- The Toxic Substances Control Act (TSCA), which authorizes the USEPA to control the manufacture, use, storage, distribution, or disposal of toxic chemicals that have the potential to leach into groundwater.

- The Clean Water Act, which authorizes the USEPA to make grants to the states for the development of groundwater protection strategies and authorizes a number of programs to prevent water pollution.

- The Safe Drinking Water Act, which also requires the USEPA to regulate underground disposal of wastes in deep wells.

Although these are all national laws, they have been designed for implementation by the states in cooperation with local government. A major reason for emphasizing local action is that groundwater protection generally involves specific decisions on land use. Local authorities given regulatory power through state statutes and sometimes regional agreements implement most land use controls.

State-level Aquifer Protection

All states have passed some type of legislation related to the protection of aquifers. This legislation falls into a number of subject areas. Some states have minimal programs, whereas others have very comprehensive ones. State water utility associations are generally active in promoting protective legislation. General features of state programs are as follows:

- *Comprehensive planning* is a program that many states have required for local jurisdictions. Cities, towns, counties, and local districts have been mandated to develop plans that protect a state's groundwaters.

- *Groundwater classification* reviews all groundwater sources and categorizes them so that the amount of protection needed can be determined and applied.

- *Standard setting* evaluates groundwater to determine levels of contamination. It can also include required remedial action.

- *Land use management* is related to planning in that it determines whether uses can cause contamination, and, if so, then regulates those uses.

- *Funding proposals* are used to aid in contaminated water cleanup and in supplying alternative drinking water in crisis areas.

- *Agricultural chemical regulations*, which are similar to federal laws, are imposed so that these chemicals are used judiciously.

- *Underground storage regulations* are imposed to control possible leakage of hazardous material that is generally stored underground. The regulations establish criteria for the registration, construction, installation, monitoring, repair, abandonment, and financial liability related to underground storage.

- *Water usage control* is exercised to allocate the use of water, with the goal of preventing saltwater intrusions or other over-utilization problems.

State programs are the most valuable general aids to the water utility. All water utility managers should ensure that there is adequate funding of state programs to protect all waters of their state.

Wellhead Protection Programs

In addition to the resources available to the utility at the national and state levels, a wellhead protection program (WHPP) adds control at the local level. If at all possible, water utilities should lead in developing the WHPP that involves their groundwater sources. The 1986 amendments to the SDWA require that each state develop a comprehensive WHPP, but that program largely depends on active participation at the local level. For information indicating the status of USEPA-approved WHPPs as of September 1998, see the following USEPA Web site: http://www.epa.gov/safewater/protect/gwr/report.htm#Appendix B.

A WHPP requires cooperation between the local civil authority and the water utility. A utility that leads this process is much more likely to be pleased with the outcome than one that has a WHPP imposed on it. The most important technical step is determination of the recharge area, as discussed previously. It is likely that the utility will have to use its own budget for funding this effort.

Determination of the wellhead protection area

There are different ways to delineate an area that needs protection, and engineering or geological consultants have their own preferences as to which method does the best job. The state health, environmental, or geological agency that is responsible for WHPPs can give valuable suggestions. Private consulting firms provide services that utilize techniques ranging from the less accurate (but also less expensive) fixed radius methods to the more accurate (but also more expensive) analytical or numerical models. Details and examples of delineation methods are available from the USEPA. Figure 7–5 illustrates a wellhead protection area laid out on a topographic map. Numerical modeling is a technique that is highly successful in some situations. Based on parameters that include hydraulic conductivity, specific yield, and streambed permeability, a computer model can be developed. This model can then be verified and modified after comparison with known events. The modeling stages might be as follows:

1. Select the study area and model grid.
2. Prepare data.
3. Calibrate the model.
4. Verify the model.
5. Check the model sensitivity.

Once a wellhead protection area has been delineated, a determination should be made of the time of travel for percolating water to reach the well. The utility should be more concerned about possible pollution in a zone that has 30 days' travel time than one that has 500 days.

Conducting a contaminant source inventory

The second step in the WHPP is to conduct a contaminant source inventory. This can begin with a paper search in the phone book; chamber of commerce files; or police, fire, and other civil authority records. After the inventory is compiled, volunteers or trained personnel can conduct fieldwork to obtain more specifics on particular contaminant sources.

Wellhead protection area management

The WHPA and the contaminant sources and future development must then be managed. Local zoning can be of immense help in doing this. Citizens, authorities, and business and industrial leaders should be informed of the importance of protecting the water supply and then asked to enact zoning laws that will control land use. Management of existing hazards can best be handled through personal contact and public education. The installation of monitoring wells may be necessary to

Legend:

🌑 Public Water Supply Well

— — — Wellhead Protection Area Using Fixed Radius

▬ ▬ ▬ Wellhead Protection Area Using Simplified Computer Program

1,000   0   2,000   3,000

scale (feet)

Source: Protecting Local Ground-Water Supplies Through Wellhead Protection *(1991).*

FIGURE 7–5 A wellhead protection area laid out on a topographic map

ensure that major industries are not causing groundwater pollution. Some utilities have even convinced these industries to install the monitoring wells and pay for the sampling.

Contingency plan

A WHPP is not complete until a contingency plan is prepared, detailing the steps to be taken if contamination ever occurs. The plan should provide for an alternative water supply for both short-term and long-term emergencies.

Continuing review

Finally, the WHPP should be an active program. Built-in review periods with short intervals for minor review and longer periods for major review should be written into the plan.

SURFACE WATER PROTECTION

As an example of the comprehensive nature of surface water protection, the Massachusetts Watershed Protection Plan provides the following statement, which applies to all watersheds, regardless of whether or not the water utility will be filtering the water:

> The protection of watersheds for ensuring the public's right to clean drinking water will require some creative and innovative approaches involving the cooperation of local, regional, and state levels of government. No agency alone can achieve the ambitious objectives required, because watersheds cover expansive areas, often encompassing several communities, and often include bordering states. Therefore, it will be in the public interest that all interested parties participate at each level of government and develop the cooperative mechanisms locally, regionally, and at the state level. The issue will be our greatest challenge and our greatest threat.

Watershed Resource Protection Plan

A watershed resource protection plan (WRPP) generally consists of the following elements:

- a description of the watershed,
- identification of watershed characteristics and activities that are present and could be detrimental to water quality,
- an assessment of the risks and how best to control detrimental activities and events,

- how detrimental activities and events should be monitored,
- determination of land ownership and what agreements are needed to control detrimental activities, and
- how best to manage and operate the program.

The watershed description includes both a set of maps and a narrative description. The base map is a USGS 1:24,000 map and has the following accompanying overlays of plastic sheeting, on which different information is drawn:

Base map	The watershed boundary
Overlay 1	Identification of points of water withdrawal and an outline of aquifers that have the potential to yield more than 100,000 gpd (380,000 L/d)
Overlay 2	Areas that have high erosion potential and information on animal populations
Overlay 3	Identification of any state groundwater discharges having state or federal permits, all surface water discharges having National Pollution Discharge Elimination System (NPDES) permits, and solid waste facilities
Overlay 4	An outline of all sewered areas
Overlay 5	Location of all gasoline stations and petroleum storage facilities and pipelines
Overlay 6	Floodplains, wetlands, streams, and water bodies
Overlay 7	Generalized land use, such as

- residential areas
- industrial areas
- commercial areas
- mixed urban areas
- croplands, orchards, golf courses
- animal-rearing areas
- other agriculture
- vacant or undeveloped land
- transportation facilities

Overlay 8   Hazardous-waste sites

Overlay 9   Water quality monitoring sites

Overlay 10   Land ownership
- open space owned or under the control of the water supplier or state, county, or municipal government
- lands in conservation restrictions in perpetuity
- all lands owned or restricted by written agreements or deed restrictions with landowners

The benefit of transparent overlay maps as a watershed-planning tool becomes evident once two or more of them have been superimposed on each other. They graphically show how the various potential problems coincide with each other. Once these maps have been used for watershed protection, they can be used for other purposes. Many government agencies and utilities are now using geographic information systems (GIS) to display these various overlays on computer-generated interactive maps. For more information on this topic, refer to *Water Transmission and Distribution*, also part of this series.

It is unlikely that this project can be done without expert help and without spending a considerable amount of money. However, watershed planning is essential if a utility wishes to receive a waiver for the surface water filtration requirements of the SDWA. Under the 1996 amendments to the SDWA, the state, with USEPA concurrence, can waive filtration requirements if a watershed is undeveloped, uninhabited, or in consolidated ownership and has access that is controlled. A watershed in this pristine condition must produce water of a quality higher than if it had been filtered and chlorinated. If the utility believes that the chances of a filtration waiver are good, the cost of watershed planning will be small compared with the cost of constructing filtration facilities. A reference to the goals of a state watershed control plan developed to help water sources to qualify for a filtration waiver is included in the last section of this chapter.

Sanitary Surveys

One of the most important control measures that any water utility can use to determine how well it is serving the public is the sanitary survey. A sanitary survey is an onsite review of the water source, facilities, equipment, operation, and maintenance of a public water system. It serves to evaluate the adequacy of all aspects of producing and distributing drinking water.

A sanitary survey of each water source is necessary for proper water source management. The utility may conduct it by following a standard form supplied by the state health authority. The form should be designed to identify all areas of concern within the supply system, including the entire watershed or aquifer recharge area. A qualified person, preferably a sanitary engineer or someone of equivalent training, should complete this portion of the form. The survey should determine the potential for contamination of the supply. This includes surveying all installations, activities, and contamination sources.

The survey, which is conducted periodically, should include water sampling at places considered significant and representative to establish a baseline for future comparison. Some portions of the system should be surveyed annually and others at less frequent intervals. Important changes in water quality found in annual sampling should be investigated. If the reason for the change cannot readily be determined, a complete survey should be performed.

Watershed Control Programs

Managing watersheds to maintain or enhance water quality is a particular necessity for utilities that wish to avoid filtration. It should, however, be a goal for all utilities using surface water. Water utility managers must eliminate obvious water quality hazards, including sewage outfalls or toxic waste and landfill drainage. In fact, continuing contaminant release on a watershed, though it may appear to be causing little or no damage, can be more dangerous in the long run. Table 7–3 lists some of the program elements for selected utility source management programs and illustrates the extensive watershed control program implemented by some water utilities.

Complete control

The ideal situation from the standpoint of water source protection is a completely fenced, utility-owned watershed. This is usually not possible, but both Seattle, Wash., and Portland, Ore., have this type of controlled supply.

Utilities that do not own an appreciable percentage of their watershed must develop different protection strategies that rely more on the cooperation of the public, the local civil authorities, and the state. An example is the Portland, Maine, Water District, which serves a relatively small population but has a 450-mi^2 (1,166-km^2) watershed that includes portions of 21 communities (Figure 7–6).

The district makes a distinction between water that flows directly to Sebago Lake and water that reaches the lake after passing through other lakes and ponds.

TABLE 7–3 Elements of source water management programs for selected surface systems with highly protected managed watersheds

	Seattle, Wash.	Portland, Ore.	New York City, N.Y.	Boston, Mass.	Bridgeport Hydraulic Company, Conn.	Hackensack Water Company, N.J.
Type of supply	Reservoir, river	Reservoir, river	Reservoir	Reservoir, river	Reservoir	Reservoir
Safe yield, mgd (ML/d)	170 (643)	108 (409)	1,290 (4,883)	300 (1,136)	66 (250)	125 (473)
Filtered	No	No	No	No	Partial	Yes
Watershed area, mi² (km²)	162 (420)	106 (275)	1,928 (4,994)	474 (1,228)	96 (249)	113 (293)
Program Elements						
Watershed owned or controlled, mi² (km²)	156 (404)	106 (275)	138(+)* (357)*	180 (466)	26 (67)	10 (26)
%	100	100	7(+)	38	27	9
In situ treatment						
Aeration	—	—	—	—	X	—
Algicide or herbicide	—	—	X	X	X	X
Wildlife control	X	Partial	—	Partial	Partial	—
Forest management	X	X	X	X	X	—
Emergency response	X	X	X	X	X	X

Table continued next page

176

TABLE 7-3 Elements of source water management programs for selected surface systems with highly protected managed watersheds (continued)

	Seattle, Wash.	Portland, Ore.	New York City, N.Y.	Boston, Mass.	Bridgeport Hydraulic Company, Conn.	Hackensack Water Company, N.J.
Sanitary survey	X	—	X	X	X	X
Source monitoring	X	X	X	X	X	X
Watershed inspection	X	X	X	X	X	X
Security patrol	X	X	X	X	X	X
Fencing	—	Partial	—	Partial	—	X
Public education	X	X	—	X	X	X

Source: Water Quality and Treatment *(1990).*

* Approximately one half of watershed dedicated to forest preserves.

Sebago Lake Watershed
Direct and Indirect Watersheds

Bethel

Greenwood

Mason

Albany

Stoneham

Norway

Lovell

Waterford

Direct Watershed

Indirect Watershed

N

6 mi (9.6 km)

Sweden

Harrison

Brighton

Otisfield

Poland

Denmark

Naples

Casco

Raymond

Sebago

Sebago
Lake

Gray

Hiram

Baldwin

Windham

State of
Maine

Standish

Watershed Location

Source: Portland Water District, Portland, Maine.

FIGURE 7–6 Sebago Lake watershed, Portland (Maine) Water District, which includes portions of 21 communities

The distinction is made because the latter water receives some beneficial treatment in reducing phosphorus and other compounds. Portland's definitions for this distinction are as follows:

- *Direct watershed* consists of all land that drains directly to a lake without passing through another lake or pond.
- *Indirect watershed* of a lake consists of all watersheds of upstream lakes and ponds.

The Portland, Maine, source protection program calls on portions of 20 federal, state, and local laws. In addition, 10 to 15 sets of rules and regulations that carry the force of law are implemented when necessary. In most cases, when the need arises to invoke a state law, the appropriate state agency will take the lead in approaching the violator. The same is true for local problems—if the utility's watershed inspector finds a malfunctioning septic system, the local plumbing inspector or code enforcement officer is contacted to see that corrections are made.

Local support

Very few utilities have police power; consequently, it becomes imperative for a utility to receive support from the authorities that do have the power. The best way to ensure this support is to have the backing of the public. Most citizens are aware of the environmental threats to water bodies and are willing to support the enforcement through corrective action. If it is "their" lake, water supply, or livelihood at stake, the public will readily help the utility.

As a result, public education is a vital part of a utility's source protection program. Operators should be available to talk to civil authorities serving on planning and zoning boards, service clubs and other social groups, and especially schools. Facilities should be maintained so that tours are always welcome and visitors always receive a positive impression.

Members of the news media can be valuable allies if they are convinced that watershed protection is necessary. It is the task of the utility to seek out newspaper, radio, and television sources so that an alliance can be forged. If the utility does not have someone on the staff capable of doing this, a public relations firm can be hired to foster a cooperative relationship between the water company, the media, and ultimately the public.

Watershed protective districts

Special watershed protective districts are another mechanism that has proven very effective in protecting water sources and watersheds. They are usually created when the geographical area to be protected is quite large and there are diverse interests desiring environmental protection.

One of the best known of these entities is the one that was organized to protect Lake Tahoe. This national treasure was being threatened by development and had the unusual feature of having its shoreline in two states (California and Nevada). Because of this, the protective legislation had to be passed by Congress.

In Maine, the Saco River Corridor Commission was founded by landowners for their own protection. However, the utility that uses the river as a water supply also benefits from the controls that are in place. The river extends a fairly long distance, which would be beyond the capabilities of the utility to protect if it had to act alone. However, the landowners have the power of eminent domain and the ability to level assessments.

It can be difficult to form protective districts because their scope can be quite broad and some interests do not see them as beneficial. In many cases, a water source has to be damaged or severely threatened before diverse groups perceive the threat and are willing to cooperate.

Even though these districts can help a utility by giving added protection to the watershed and water body, it may result in less control by the utility. Important decisions related to the watershed or water body, which were once made by the utility, will now be decided by a group comprised of a board of directors, of which the utility is only a one-vote member.

Land Management

In addition to the social and political aspects of watershed management, the actual practices of landowners or land users must be managed.

Forest management

A forest is a familiar and valuable feature on watersheds in much of the country. Not only do they protect water quality but also many utilities manage the forests as a source of income. Timber harvesting can be extremely damaging to the watershed and to water quality. Consequently, it is important to require that environmentally responsible tree cutters who are experienced in best management practices (BMPs) are responsible for harvesting the timber.

If the practices presently in use do not adequately protect the water source, a registered forester should be consulted. An example of going beyond ordinary practices is a requirement that horses be used for tree-cutting work because motor-powered machinery is too damaging to the forest floor.

Much the same is true of home or commercial land development. If large areas are stripped of vegetation, extreme care must be exercised to make sure that erosion of the bare land does not damage the source water. Holding ponds and sediment basins that are constructed to minimize damage should be left in place after the project is completed so that the benefits they offer can continue. Revegetation of the watershed with woody species should be encouraged so that soil stabilization and infiltration of water to recharge groundwater will develop once again.

Management of agricultural practices

Agricultural practices may or may not be conducive to wise source water protection. Farmers are usually in touch with conservation districts or extension agents (government officials who serve as consultants to agriculture), and the utility can enlist the aid of these experts to act as a liaison with the agricultural community. These experts can assist by encouraging BMPs for agricultural practice and providing general watershed education to the farmers.

Management in urban areas

Homeowners close to a water body should be informed of the harmful effects of lawn and gardening practices that are not conducted properly. The use of nitrogen and phosphorous fertilizers to turn lawns green can also turn lakes green with algae. The following list of recommendations was taken from one of the first Source Water Assessments provided to the Philadelphia Suburban Water Company through a grant from the Pennsylvania Department of Environmental Protection (Schnabel Engineering 2001). Zone A is the portion of the watershed that could transport a contaminant to the water supply intake within a 5-hour period after introduction:

- Cooperative action to label and protect storm drains and tributary systems in Zone A, including inventorying and labeling storm and roadway drains and road crossings.

- Delineation and identification of the boundary of Zone A on township and borough zoning maps.

- Enactment of ordinances that require measures to infiltrate or retain and treat stormwater runoff to remove sediment and nutrients and capture potential spills (particularly in Zone A); as well as ordinances that might encourage retrofitting of existing storm drains and road drains to protect source water, including measures to protect and restore forested riparian buffers.

- Grant funds or loan programs to commercial/industrial/residential areas to pay for improvements to stormwater management facilities.

- Retrofitting by the Department of Transportation of drainage systems from state highways that drain directly into tributaries of Zone A.

- Improved management of septic systems.

- Improved monitoring and/or instrumentation of sewer collector systems and lift stations, particularly in Zone A.
- Adoption and implementation of Act 537 wastewater facilities plans to accommodate future growth while addressing issues of failing septic systems and to preserve (and if possible, enhance) quality and quantity of water in both Zone A and Zone B.
- Cooperative action to control Canada geese and other waterfowl on the watershed, particularly within Zone A.
- Cooperative streambank and forested riparian corridor restoration projects.

Management of transportation facilities

If highways or railroads run through or close to water bodies, the emergency response agencies, namely police and fire departments, should know the proper procedure for dealing with spills. Flushing the contents of a serious spill off the highway to prevent fire or traffic disruption could put a water system out of business. For example, if a fire department uses water to extinguish a fire in an agricultural supply warehouse, they will probably flush pesticides and other chemicals into a nearby stream. They can usually contain the fire just as well with misting and allow the fire to burn itself out.

Recreational Use of Lakes and Reservoirs

Recreational use of water supply reservoirs or lakes has long been a subject of controversy. Studies have shown that controlled recreational use has minimal impact. However, water system managers generally have an aversion to the public being given free rein on water bodies that are used as drinking water sources because of the liability if anything goes wrong.

Because of population pressures from urban areas and the desirability of outdoor activities (especially those involving water), it is difficult to deny the public some use of watershed land. The goal then becomes one of managing recreational uses so that they do not threaten water quality.

Levels of recreational use

The following descriptions of recreational use range from a very low level of human activity to the very highest level. Many water utilities do not have the luxury of returning a watershed or water body to a low level of human contact if full recreational use is presently taking place.

The least impact on water quality occurs when recreation can be limited to bike and hiking paths, nature walks, and picnic areas. Even with these activities, it is necessary to provide adequate, clean, attractive toilet facilities and a plentiful supply of waste disposal containers that are serviced on a regular basis.

The above activities, plus fishing from shores and boats, form the next least-harmful recreational activity level. Boats should have no motors or small, electrically powered motors. Launch sites should be as far from intake structures as possible, and restricted zones should be designated around intakes and marked with buoys.

The next level is to have less restriction on fishing and to allow boats with greater horsepower for nonfishing recreation. Speeds should be controlled to prevent erosion from wakes and to promote safety. Again, restricted areas should be enforced, and waste tanks on boats should be sealed so that wastes must be pumped out at an approved facility. Onshore sanitary facilities for people and boat holding-tank flushing stations should be provided. Fuel for boats should be kept as secure and free from spillage as possible.

Bodily contact with the water is the last level in this progression. Public swimming areas should be kept as far as possible from intake structures. Good onshore sanitary facilities should also be provided.

In all of these different scenarios, water quality monitoring and sanitary inspection are a necessity. It is obvious that as human contact increases, the more stringent the monitoring requirements become. If serious bacterial degradation occurs, regulators should be asked to help restrict activities.

Land erosion

Erosion of watershed land adjacent to the shore of streams and lakes seems to be the most important threat to water quality. It can result from footpaths and bike paths, but it can be much more serious with motor vehicles. Automobiles and trucks are an obvious cause for erosion, yet the most serious threat comes from motorbikes, motorcycles, and all-terrain vehicles. Both on- and off-trail uses cause impacts to vegetative cover and compression of the soil surface. Overcompaction of soils, especially on slopes, ultimately results in serious soil losses during precipitation events when overland or sheet flow takes place. Therefore, use of off-road vehicles near shorelines of streams and lakes should be discouraged, as well as overuse of paths that are unprotected by gravel or wood chips.

Finally, loss of soil due to erosion within stream channels results in transport of heavy sediment loads into a drinking water reservoir. Heavy sediment loads decrease water quality as well as result in the loss of volume storage of water. Revegetation of stream banks and contiguous areas damaged by recreational activities should be a priority management effort within a surface drinking water watershed. In addition, limiting high flow velocity within the entire stream channel network would lessen the impacts caused by soil erosion.

Recreational fees

Another concept that has generally been accepted is that the public is more likely to follow the rules if they are charged for the use. Fees can also make the management of recreation on watersheds and water bodies less costly and thus more acceptable to taxpayers or customers. Care has to be taken, however, not to exclude those less able to pay.

Other concerns

Many potential threats to source water quality remain but have not been addressed here. Adherence to sound watershed management practices by civil and public authorities as well as vigilance on the part of the utility will foster maintenance of high raw water quality at the intake. The discussion of recreation applies only to raw water sources. Recreation on finished water reservoirs, which is universally discouraged by the American Water Works Association and state health authorities, should be completely prohibited.

Source Water Protection for Filtration Waiver Attainment

A well-defined watershed control plan is mandatory for a utility to receive a waiver for filtration as required by the Surface Water Treatment Rule. Although filtration waivers are part of the national SDWA, the states that have assumed primacy have considerable flexibility in determining how the provisions will be enforced. The following information related to avoiding surface water filtration is part of the Massachusetts Watershed Protection Plan. Other states have similar plans. The plan's policy goals are as follows:

1. Provide guidance to water suppliers for preparing and submitting a report that describes a watershed control plan that will meet the USEPA's SDWA requirements to avoid mandatory filtration and to serve as a watershed protection plan.

2. Provide specific and consistent guidance for the protection, preservation, and improvement of raw water quality of surface water supplies. (These sources are open to the atmosphere and subject to surface runoff, or they may be groundwaters that originate from a surface water supply.)

3. Provide a comprehensive approach to identify and control existing and potential sources of pollution of surface water supplies.

4. Link land use activities to water quality concerns, and ensure that a consistent set of standards and safeguards are applied for reducing vulnerability to contamination from inappropriate land uses.

5. Encourage cooperation among the water supplier, landowners, and local authorities sharing a resource area to set up agreements to control discharges to the environment and to respond to emergencies.

6. Provide for an ongoing monitoring program that will be used by the state Department of Environmental Protection to determine the effectiveness of the watershed controls on raw water quality.

SELECTED SUPPLEMENTARY READINGS

Black, P.E. 1996. *Watershed Hydrology, 2nd ed.* Chelsea, Mich.: Sleeping Bear Press.

Citizens' Guide to Ground-Water Protection. 1990. Washington, D.C.: US Environmental Protection Agency, Office of Drinking Water.

Cooke, G.D., and R.E. Carlson. *Reservoir Management for Water Quality and THM Precursor Control.* 1989. Denver, Colo.: Awwa Research Foundation and American Water Works Association.

Drinking Water Quality Enhancement Through Source Protection. 1977. Ann Arbor, Mich.: Ann Arbor Science.

Dunne, T., and L.B. Leopold. 1978. *Water in Environmental Planning.* San Francisco, Calif.: W.H. Freeman and Company.

Guide for Conducting Contaminant Source Inventories for Public Drinking Water Supplies. 1991. Washington, D.C.: US Environmental Protection Agency, Office of Drinking Water.

Local Financing for Wellhead Protection. 1989. Washington, D.C.: US Environmental Protection Agency, Office of Drinking Water.

Massachusetts Watershed Protection Plan. Boston, Mass.: Department of Environmental Protection.

Pennsylvania Department of Environmental Protection. 2000. *Source Water Assessment and Protection Program.* Document No. 383-5000-001. Harrisburg, Pa.: Pennsylvania Department of Environmental Protection.

Protecting Local Ground-Water Supplies Through Wellhead Protection. 1991. Washington, D.C.: US Environmental Protection Agency, Office of Drinking Water.

Robbins, R.W., J.L. Glicker, D.M. Bloem, and B.M. Niss. 1991. *Effective Watershed Management for Surface Water Supplies.* Denver, Colo.: Awwa Research Foundation and American Water Works Association.

Schnabel Engineering Associates, Inc. 2001. *Source Water Assessment, Public Summary Crum Creek Basin—Philadelphia Suburban Water Company, October 2001.* Unpublished public document, Schnabel Engineering Associates, West Chester, Pa.

Stewart, J.C. 1990. *Drinking Water Hazards.* Hiram, Ohio: Envirographics.

Symons, J.M., M.E. Whitworth, P.B. Bedient, and J.G. Haughton. 1989. Managing an Urban Watershed. *Jour. AWWA,* 81(8):30.

Water Quality and Treatment, 5th ed. 1999. New York: McGraw-Hill and American Water Works Association (available from AWWA).

Wellhead Protection—A Decision Makers' Guide. 1987. Washington, D.C.: US Environmental Protection Agency, Office of Ground Water Protection.

Winter, T.C., J.W. Harvey, O.L. Franke, and W.M. Alley. 1998. *Ground Water and Surface Water: A Single Resource.* Circular 1139. Denver, Colo.: US Geological Survey.

Glossary

absolute ownership   A water rights term referring to water that is completely owned by one person.

absolute right   A water right that cannot be abridged.

acid rain   Rain or snow that has a low pH because of atmospheric contamination.

acidic water   Water having a pH less than 7.0.

adsorption   A physical process in which molecules adhere to a substance because of electrical charges.

advanced wastewater treatment   The treatment of sewage beyond the ordinary level of treatment.

aeration   The process of bringing water and air into close contact to remove or modify constituents in the water.

aesthetic   Of or pertaining to the senses.

air-stripping   Removal of a substance from water by means of air.

algae   Primitive plants (one- or many-celled) that usually live in water and are capable of obtaining their food by photosynthesis.

alkaline water   Water having a pH greater than 7.0. Also called *basic water*.

alluvial   Referring to a type of soil, mostly sand and gravel, deposited by flowing water.

anaerobic   Occurring in the absence of air or free oxygen.

annual average daily flow   The average of the daily flows for a 12-month period. It may be determined by means of dividing the total volume of water for the year by 365, the number of days in the year.

annular space   The space between the outside of a well casing and the drilled hole.

appropriation doctrine   A water rights doctrine in which the first user has right to water before subsequent users.

appropriation–permit system   A water use system in which permits to use water are regulated so that overdraft cannot occur.

appropriative rights   Water rights acquired by means of diverting and putting the water to beneficial use following procedures established by state statutes or courts.

aquatic life   All forms of animal and plant life that live in water.

aqueduct   A conduit, usually of considerable size, used to convey water.

aquifer   A porous, water-bearing geologic formation. Generally restricted to materials capable of yielding an appreciable supply of water. Also called *groundwater aquifer.*

aquifer recharge area   The land above an aquifer that contributes water to it.

artesian aquifer   An aquifer in which the water is confined by both an upper and a lower impermeable layer.

artesian well   A well in which water pressure forces water up through a hole in the upper confining, or impermeable, layer of an artesian aquifer. In a flowing artesian well, the water will rise to the ground surface and flow out onto the ground.

artificial wetland   A wet area created by either damming or rerouting a stream and/or grading down to groundwater, eventually resulting in the growth of wetland plants, and the development of wetland hydrology and hydric soils.

atmospheric deposition   The process whereby airborne particles and gases are deposited on the earth's surface.

atom   The basic structural unit of matter; the smallest particle of an element that can combine chemically with similar particles of the same or other elements to form molecules of a compound.

average daily flow   The sum of all daily flows for a specified time period, divided by the number of daily flows added.

bacteria   A group of one-celled microscopic organisms that have no chlorophyll. Usually have spherical, rodlike, or curved shapes. Usually regarded as plants.

basic water   See *alkaline water.*

beneficial use   A water rights term indicating that the water is being used for good purposes.

biofilm   A layer of biological material that covers a surface.

bloom   An undesirable large growth of algae or diatoms in a lake or water reservoir.

buffered   Able to resist changes in pH.

caisson   A large-diameter excavated chamber in which work can be done beneath the surface of the earth or water.

capillary action   The degree to which a material or object containing minute openings or passages, when immersed in a liquid, usually water, will draw the surface of the liquid above the water surface.

carcinogenic   Capable of causing cancer.

casing   (1) The enclosure surrounding a pump impeller, into which are machined the suction and discharge ports. (2) The metal pipe used to line the borehole of a well (also called *well casing*).

cement grout   A mixture of cement and water used to seal openings in well construction.

chemical oxidation   The use of a chemical, such as chlorine or ozone, to remove or change some contaminant in water.

chemical precipitation   The use of a chemical to cause some contaminant to become insoluble in water.

chlorophyll   The green matter in plants or algae.

coagulation   A treatment that causes particles in water to adhere to each other to form larger particles.

coliform group   A group of bacteria predominantly inhabiting the intestines of humans or animals, but also occasionally found elsewhere. Presence of the bacteria in water is used as an indication of fecal contamination (contamination by human or animal waste).

color   A physical characteristic describing the appearance of water that is other than clear. Different from *turbidity*, which is the cloudiness of water.

color units (cu)   The unit of measure used to express the color of a water sample.

commercial water uses   Use of water in business activities such as motels, shopping centers, gas stations, and laundries.

common-law doctrine   Laws that are a part of a large body of civil law that, for the most part, was made by judges in court decisions (rather than being enacted by a legislative body).

compaction   A process that renders soil more dense and often reduces water transfer.

comprehensive planning   A process that results in widespread community planning.

computer model   A means of defining a system using computer programs.

condensation   The process by which a substance changes from the gaseous form to a liquid or solid form. Water that falls as precipitation from the atmosphere has condensed from the vapor (gaseous) state to rain or snow. Dew and frost are also forms of condensation on the surface of the earth or vegetation.

cone of depression   The cone-shaped depression in the groundwater level around a well during pumping.

confining bed   A layer of material, typically consolidated rock or clay, that has very low permeability and restricts the movement of groundwater into or out of adjacent aquifers.

consecutive systems   Two or more water systems that take water from a single providing system.

conservation district   A governmental entity that acts to protect soil and water.

contaminant source inventory   A record of the activities on a watershed or aquifer recharge area that have a potential to contaminate water.

contaminant   Anything found in water other than hydrogen or oxygen.

contamination   Any introduction into water of microorganisms, chemicals, wastes, or wastewater in a concentration that makes the water unfit for its intended use.

contingency plan   A document that details the action of a water utility under specified adverse conditions.

corrosion   Destruction by chemical action.

curbs   Precast concrete liners for dug wells.

cyst   A resistant form of a living organism.

daily flow   The total volume of water (in gallons or liters) passing through a plant during a 24-hour period.

demand factor   The ratio of the peak or minimum demand to the average demand.

demand management   A conservation term that refers to controlling the users' use of water.

density stratification   The formation of layers of water in a reservoir, with the water that is the densest at the bottom and least dense at the surface.

detention time   The period for which water is held before some further action takes place.

disinfection   The water treatment process that kills disease-causing organisms in water, usually by adding chlorine.

dissolved oxygen (DO)   The oxygen dissolved in water, wastewater, or other liquid, usually expressed in milligrams per liter, parts per million, or percent of saturation.

dissolved solids   Any material that is dissolved in water and can be recovered by evaporating the water after filtering the suspended material.

divide   The line that follows the ridges or summits forming the boundary of a drainage basin (watershed) and that separates one drainage basin from another. Also called *watershed divide*.

drainage basin   An area from which surface runoff is carried away by a single drainage system. Also called *catchment area* or *watershed drainage area*.

drawdown   The difference between the static water level and the pumping water level in a well.

drawdown method   A testing procedure to determine the characteristics of an aquifer or well.

dual system   A double system of pipelines, one carrying potable water and the other water of lesser quality.

effluent   Water flowing out of a structure such as a treatment plant.

electrical conductivity (EC)   A test that measures the ability of water to transmit electricity. Electrical conductivity is an indicator of dissolved solids concentration. Normally an EC of 1,000 μmhos per square centimeter indicates a dissolved solids concentration of 600–700 mg/L.

eminent domain   The power to seize property.

ephemeral stream (1) A stream that flows only in direct response to precipitation. Such a stream receives no water from springs and no continued supply from melting snow or other surface source. Its channel is above the water table at all times. (2) Streams or stretches of streams that do not flow continuously during periods of as much as 1 month.

Escherichia coli (E. coli) A bacterial species; one of the fecal coliforms.

eutrophication A process by which a lake produces too many single-celled algae cells resulting from the input of the nutrients, which cause their excessive growth. A eutrophying water body is usually characterized by a marked decrease in water clarity, oxygen depletion during the night, and a general decrease in water quality.

evaporation The process by which water becomes a vapor at a temperature below the boiling point. The rate of evaporation is generally expressed in inches or centimeters per day, month, or year.

evapotranspiration The evaporative loss of water from the earth's surface combined with losses from transpiration by plants and evaporation of water intercepted by plants and objects.

extension agents Government officials who serve as consultants to agriculture.

fecal coliform A bacterial group that is an indicator of human or animal pollution.

filterable residue test A test used to measure the total dissolved solids in water by first filtering out any undissolved solids and then evaporating the filtered water to dryness. The residue that remains is called *filterable residue* or *total dissolved solids*.

filtration The process of removing solids from water by passing the water through some material or device.

flotation A process for separating solids from water by using air to float the particles.

flow General term for movement of water, commonly used to mean (imprecisely) instantaneous flow rate, average flow rate, or volume.

flow rate The volume of water passing by a point per unit of time. Flow rates are either instantaneous or average.

frazil ice Small ice crystals that can block water intakes.

free residual chlorine Hypochlorous acid in water that responds to testing procedures and that serves as an active disinfectant.

geographic information system (GIS)   A computer hardware and software system that captures, analyzes, and displays interrelated and geographically linked data.

Giardia lamblia   A protozoan that can survive in water and that causes human disease.

granular activated carbon   A chemical used to remove certain dissolved contaminants from water.

granular media   A material used for filtering water, consisting of grains of sand or other material.

gravel pack   Gravel surrounding the well intake screen, artificially placed ("packed") to aid the screen in filtering out the sand of an aquifer. Needed only in aquifers containing a large proportion of fine-grained material.

groundwater   Subsurface water occupying the saturation zone, from which wells and springs are fed. In a strict sense, the term applies only to water below the water table.

groundwater aquifer   See *aquifer*.

groundwater classification   A scheme to categorize groundwater according to its quality.

hardness   A characteristic of water, caused primarily by the salts of calcium and magnesium. Causes deposition of scale in boilers, damage in some industrial processes, and sometimes objectionable taste. May also decrease the effectiveness of soap.

hazardous-waste facilities   Depository areas where dangerous materials are stored.

hydraulic conductivity   A measure of the ease with which water will flow through geologic formations.

hydraulic jetting   The use of water forced through the well screen to suspend fine particles in well development.

hydraulics   The branch of science that deals with fluids at rest and in motion.

hydric soils   Soils that are either saturated or ponded long enough to be depleted of oxygen for extended periods. Hydric soils are found in wetlands and other water bodies.

hydrodynamics   The study of water in motion.

hydrologic cycle   The water cycle; the movement of water to and from the surface of the earth.

hydrology   The science dealing with the properties, distribution, and circulation of water and its constituents in the atmosphere, on the earth's surface, and below the earth's surface.

hydrostatics   The study of water at rest.

impermeable layer   A layer not allowing, or allowing only with great difficulty, the movement of water.

impervious   Resistant to the passage of water.

impoundment   A pond, lake, tank, basin, or other space that is used for storage, regulation, and control of water.

indicator organisms   A bacterium that does not cause disease but indicates that disease-causing bacteria may be present. See *fecal coliform*.

indirect potable reuse   The use of water from streams that have upstream discharges of wastewater.

industrial water use   Use of water in industrial activities such as power generation, steel manufacturing, pulp and paper processing, and food processing.

infiltration   The flow or movement of water through soil.

infiltration gallery   A subsurface structure to receive water filtered through a stream bed.

inorganic material   Chemical substances of mineral origin, or more correctly, not of basically carbon structure.

instantaneous flow rate   The flow rate (volume per time) at any instant. Defined by the equation $Q = AV$, where Q = flow rate, A = cross-sectional area of the water, and V = velocity.

intake structure   A structure or device placed in a surface water source to permit the withdrawal of water from that source.

interception   The interruption of precipitation by an object on the earth's surface that limits it from reaching the ground surface; usually leaves and stems of vegetation in undevelped watersheds, buildings and roads in developed watersheds.

ion exchange   A process that removes undesirable chemicals from water and replaces them with harmless ones.

maximum contaminant level (MCL) The maximum permissible level of a contaminant in water as specified in the regulations of the Safe Drinking Water Act.

membrane processes Water purification processes using thin plastic films.

milligrams per liter (mg/L) A unit of the concentration of water or wastewater constituents. One mg/L is equivalent to 0.001 g of the constituent in 1,000 mL (1 L) of water. For reporting the results of water and wastewater analyses, this unit has replaced parts per million, to which it is approximately equivalent.

minimum day The day during which the minimum-day demand occurs.

minimum-day demand Least volume per day flowing through the plant for any day of the year.

minimum-hour demand Least volume per hour flowing through a plant for any hour in the year.

minimum-month demand Least volume of water passing through the plant during a calendar month.

molecule The smallest particle of a compound that has the compound's characteristics.

mrem Millirem. See *rem*.

National Pollution Discharge Elimination System (NPDES) A licensing system for waste discharges.

nephelometric turbidity unit (ntu) The unit of measure used to express the turbidity (cloudiness) of a water sample.

nitrogen fertilizer A plant nutrient that can cause algae blooms in sensitive water bodies.

nonpoint sources Material entering a water body that comes from overland flow or groundwater discharge rather than out of a pipe.

numerical modeling A computerized technique for determining an aquifer recharge area.

observation well Well placed near a production well to monitor changes in the aquifer.

organic adsorption The removal of volatile organic chemicals and synthetic organic chemicals by use of activated carbon.

organic material Chemicals that contain carbon and are associated with living matter.

overlay maps Transparent sheets containing data that are placed over the base map and indicate special features.

overlying use The land use that occurs on top of an aquifer.

oxidant A chemical that oxidizes other materials.

oxidize To chemically combine with oxygen, or in the case of bacteria or other organics, the combination of oxygen and organic material to form more stable organics or minerals.

oxygen depletion A state in which oxygen has been used up so that little or none is left.

ozone A form of oxygen that has very strong oxidizing powers.

palatable Pleasing to the taste.

parts per million (ppm) Unit of measure indicating the number of weight or volume units of a constituent present for each 1 million units of the solution or mixture. Formerly used to express the results of most water and wastewater analyses, but recently replaced by the use of milligrams per liter.

pathogens Disease-causing organisms.

peak day The day during which the peak-day demand occurs.

peak-day demand The greatest volume per day flowing through a plant for any day of the year.

peak-hour demand The greatest volume per hour flowing through a plant for any hour in the year.

peak-month demand The greatest volume of water passing through the plant during a calendar month.

percolation The downward movement or flow of water through the pores of soil once filtration has occurred.

perennial stream A stream that flows continuously at all seasons of a year and during dry as well as wet years. Such a stream is usually fed by groundwater, and its water surface generally stands at a lower level than that of the water table in the locality.

pH   A measure of the acidic or alkaline nature of water. Values of pH range from 1 (most acidic) to 14 (most alkaline); pure water, which is neutral (neither acidic nor alkaline), has a pH of 7, the center of the range.

phosphorus fertilizer   A plant nutrient that can cause algae blooms in sensitive water bodies.

photochemical oxidation   Changes in chemicals caused by sunlight.

photosynthesis   The process by which plants, using the chemical chlorophyll, convert the energy of the sun into food energy. Through photosynthesis, all plants and ultimately all animals (which feed on plants or other, plant-eating animals) obtain the energy of life from sunlight.

piezometric surface   The surface that coincides with the static water level in an artesian aquifer.

point source   Water potentially containing contaminants coming from a discharge pipe.

police power   The ability to enforce laws.

pollution   A condition created by the presence of harmful or objectionable material in water.

poorly buffered   Not resisting changes in pH.

porosity   An indication of the volume of space within a given amount of a material.

powdered activated carbon   Carbon, added to water in powdered form, used to remove chemicals from water.

precipitation   The process by which atmospheric moisture is discharged onto land or water surface. Precipitation, in the form of rain, snow, hail, or sleet, is usually expressed as depth for a day, month, or year, and designated as daily, monthly, or annual precipitation.

primacy   The acceptance by states of the task of enforcing the SDWA.

priority use   The assigning of water rights based on who has been using the water the longest.

pristine   Pure and free from contamination.

protozoa   Small single-celled animals including amoebae, ciliates, and flagellates.

public water use   Use of water to support public facilities such as public buildings and offices, parks, golf courses, picnic grounds, campgrounds, and ornamental fountains.

quagga mussel   A bivalve that multiplies rapidly in fresh water and can clog intake pipes.

qualified right   A water rights term indicating that the right to water use is not absolute but must be shared with others.

radial well   A very wide, relatively shallow caisson that has horizontally drilled wells with screen points at the bottom. Radial wells are large producers.

radioactive   Referring to a material that has an unstable atomic nucleus, which spontaneously decays or disintegrates, producing radiation.

rainfall intensity   The amount of rainfall occurring during a specified time. Rainfall intensity is usually expressed as inches or centimeters per hour.

reasonable use   A water rights term indicating that the water use is acceptable in general terms.

recharge   Addition of water to the groundwater supply from precipitation and by infiltration from surface streams, lakes, reservoirs, and snowmelt.

recovery method   A procedure for aquifer evaluation that measures how quickly water levels return to normal after pumping.

rem   A unit of measure of radioactive effects on humans.

reuse water   Wastewater treated to make it useful.

riparian doctrine   A water right that allows the owners of land abutting a stream or other natural body of water to use that water.

riparians   Those whose property holdings are along the shores of a water body.

riparian zone   The area contiguous to the streambank of a flowing water body or the shoreline of an open water body like a lake or pond. This area may be an upland or wetland but is important to maintaining high water quality in the water body.

rule of correlative rights   A water rights rule specifying that rights are not absolute but depend also on the rights of others.

safe yield   The maximum dependable water supply that can be withdrawn continuously from a surface water or groundwater supply during a period of years in which the driest period or period of greatest deficiency in water supply is likely to occur.

saltwater intrusion   The invasion of an aquifer by salt water because of overpumping of a well.

sand barrier   A layer of gravel around the curb of a dug well.

sanitary survey   A detailed inspection of a facility with a view to public health concerns.

saturated   The condition of a material when it can absorb no more of a second material. Saturated soil has its void spaces completely filled with water, so any water added will run off and not soak in.

screens   A device for excluding debris on a surface water intake and for excluding sand in a groundwater supply.

SDWA   The Safe Drinking Water Act.

secondary maximum contaminant level (SMCL)   A nonenforceable regulation on a nonhealth-related contaminant.

sedimentation   A treatment process using gravity to remove coagulated particles.

seepage   The slow movement of water through small cracks or pores of a material.

service outlet   A device used for releasing water at a dam for downstream uses.

siltation   The accumulation of silt (small soil particles between 0.00016 and 0.0024 in. [0.004 and 0.061 mm] in diameter) in an impoundment.

slide gate   A device on a dam to control the release of water.

sole-source aquifer   The single water supply available in an area; also a USEPA designation for water protection.

solubilization   The process of making a material easier to dissolve.

specific-capacity method   A testing method for determining the adequacy of an aquifer or well.

specific yield   A measure of well yield per unit of drawdown.

spillway   A device used to release water from a dam.

spring   A location where groundwater emerges on the surface of the ground.

sterilization   The removal of all life from water, as contrasted with *disinfection*.

stream bed permeability   Measure of the ability of the bottom of a watercourse to transmit water to and from the underground.

stream channel   The course through which a stream flows.

supply management   The implementation of techniques by a utility to save water.

surface runoff   (1) That portion of the runoff of a drainage basin that has not percolated beneath the surface after precipitation. (2) The water that reaches a stream by traveling over the soil surface or by falling directly into the stream channels, including not only the large permanent streams but also the tiny rills and rivulets.

surface water   All water on the surface, as distinguished from *groundwater*.

surger   A device used to develop a well.

surging and bailing   A method used to develop a well by alternately increasing and decreasing water pressure against the walls of the well to dislodge small particles.

synthetic organic chemicals (SOCs)   Chemicals produced by humans that can be water contaminants.

temperature   A physical characteristic of water. The temperature of water is normally measured on one of two scales: Fahrenheit or Celsius.

thermal stratification   The layering of water as a result of temperature differences.

thermoelectric power   Electricity produced by heat in which water is used for steam production.

threshold odor   The minimum odor of a water sample that can just be detected after successive dilutions of odorless water.

threshold odor number (TON)   A numerical designation of the intensity of odor in water.

time of travel   The time required for groundwater recharge to percolate through the soil and get to the wellhead.

topographic map   A map that shows the elevation of the land in a specified area.

transpiration   The process by which water vapor is lost to the atmosphere from living plants.

trihalomethanes (THMs)   Compounds of chlorine and organic matter that are generated during disinfection.

turbidity   A physical characteristic of water making the water appear cloudy. The condition is caused by the presence of suspended matter.

turnover   The vertical circulation of water in large water bodies caused by the mixing effects of temperature changes and wind.

ultraviolet irradiation   Use of a portion of the light spectrum to disinfect drinking water.

unaccounted-for water   Water use that does not go through meters and thus is not paid for (including water that is wasted).

viruses   The smallest and simplest form of life. The many types of viruses reproduce themselves in a manner that causes infectious disease in some larger life forms, such as humans.

void spaces   A pore or open space in rock or granular material that is not occupied by solid matter. It may be occupied by air, water, or other gaseous or liquid material.

volatile organic chemicals (VOCs)   Organics that are produced by humans, are primarily solvents, and are found in water as contaminants.

waiver for filtration   An exception granted to a state so that a water source can be served without prior filtration.

water body   A natural or artificial basin in which water is impounded.

waterborne disease   A disease caused by a waterborne organism or toxic substance.

water conservation   The reduction of water usage, accomplished primarily by preventing waste.

watercourse   (1) A running stream of water. (2) A natural or artificial channel for the passage of water.

water rights   A body of law that determines water ownership.

water-saving fixtures   Devices and appliances specifically designed to have low water use.

water-saving kits   Devices sometimes distributed by utilities to reduce customer water usage.

watershed   See *drainage basin*.

watershed boundary   The watershed divide (the high point on a watershed), which directs the flow of water in a certain direction.

watershed divide   See *watershed boundary*.

water table   The upper surface of the zone of saturation closest to the ground surface.

water-table aquifer   An aquifer confined only by a lower impermeable layer.

water-table well   A well constructed in a water-table aquifer.

well development   The process of removing particles from an aquifer to produce potable water.

well field placement   The arranging of wells to achieve a desired output from an aquifer.

wellhead protection   A process of controlling potential groundwater contamination for a specific groundwater source.

wellhead protection program (WHPP)   A program required by the Safe Drinking Water Act to achieve wellhead protection.

wetland   Areas that are inundated or saturated by surface or groundwater at a frequency and duration sufficient to support, and that under normal circumstances do support, a prevalence of vegetation typically adapted for life in saturated soil conditions, including swamps, marshes, bogs, and similar areas.

Xeriscaping   The selection and use of trees, shrubs, and plants that require small amounts of water for landscaping.

zebra mussel   A bivalve that is a serious pest in surface water because it blocks intake pipes.

zone of saturation   The part of an aquifer that has all the water it can contain.

zoning   A civil process that controls land use.

Index

NOTE: *f.* indicates a figure; *t.* indicates a table.